Push-hands

The handbook for noncompetitive Tai Chi practice with a partner

Push-hands

The handbook for
noncompetitive Tai Chi
practice with a partner

Herman Kauz

THE OVERLOOK PRESS
WOODSTOCK • NEW YORK

CA(86)

JUL - - 1997

First published in the United States in 1997 by
The Overlook Press
Lewis Hollow Road
Woodstock, New York 12498

Library of Congress Cataloging-in-Publications Data

Kauz, Herman.
Push-hands : the handbook for noncompetitive Tai chi practice
with a partner / Herman Kauz.
p. cm.
1. Tai chi chuan. I. Title
GV504.K38 1997   613.7'148--dc20   96-30615
ISBN 0-89751-754-9

BOOK DESIGN AND FORMATTING BY BERNARD SCHLEIFER

Printed in the United States of America

First Edition

10 9 8 7 6 5 4 3 2 1

Contents

Acknowledgments

I WOULD LIKE TO THANK the following persons for their help in posing for the photographs: Jamie Moffett, Renate Van Zandt, Marjorie Yance and Topper Yance. The high quality of the photography is in large part due to the attention to detail of both Topper and Marjorie Yance. Finally, I am grateful for the contribution of Emiko Kauz in typing and proofreading the manuscript as well as in offering valuable suggestions of one sort or another, not all of which had to do with the book.

Push-hands

The handbook for noncompetitive
Tai Chi practice with a partner

I.
Introduction

I N THE WEST, we have in recent years become increasingly aware through the media of the value for our society of a centuries-old Chinese form of exercise and self-defense called tai chi chuan. The emphasis of most presentations is on the tai chi solo form and its usefulness as therapeutic exercise that without much strain gradually strengthens our legs, helps us to relax, and in some exotic Asian way benefits our health. Thus, the form is our first introduction to tai chi, but we should also be aware that the art includes push-hands practice with a partner, self-defense, and fighting training, and can run to proficiency in the use of various edged weapons. More importantly, our training if properly conducted will extend far beyond mere exercise and self-defense and will encompass meditative aspects that can enable us to see reality more clearly.

The general instructional pattern in tai chi chuan is for students to first learn the solo form which takes about five or six months on the basis of once-a-week hour-long sessions. The form is sequential and beginners learn a segment each week. Daily practice at home is mandatory if students are to learn the correct placement of hands, feet, and body and to internalize a tai chi way of moving and thinking.

In an attempt to help my students learn the tai chi form,

about twenty-five years ago I prepared a manual that presented the form as I had learned it from my teacher, Cheng, Man-ching. The book, *Tai Chi Handbook,* has been useful to students over the years. However, my thoughts about tai chi and its many benefits have developed further with my additional seasoning in this art. This book on push-hands goes somewhat beyond the basic ideas set down in the Handbook in an attempt to broaden and deepen students' understanding of the tai chi form and especially of push-hands.

Form correction usually follows the completion of the tai chi form; I combine form correction with an introduction to push-hands. I follow this pattern because it is the way I was taught and also because my experience has shown it to be best suited to the requirements of tai chi training. By learning the form first students have a chance, among other developments, to begin to relax, to center themselves, and to become aware of how they are using the different parts of their body. The Taoist principles employed in push-hands are less alien and more easily assimilated by students after they have practiced the tai chi form for at least six months. Over the years, I have at one time or another and for various reasons allowed students to begin pushing hands before they completed the form. The relatively few whose training was accelerated in this way did not seem either to suffer from it or to benefit additionally. But, everything considered, I believe finishing the form before learning push-hands is the optimum procedure, because it gives students a chance to learn at a slow and careful pace, to digest some of what they are learning, and to prepare themselves a bit for continuing their development with push-hands. The view in tai chi should be the long one, so there is no need to hurry.

A benefit of learning and doing the solo form before moving on to push-hands is that in individual practice we are not distracted or disturbed by the presence of a partner or opponent. We should not forget that tai chi chuan is a martial art and that the hand and body movements we practice are those we might use to defend ourselves if we came under attack. Though we train not to learn to fight but to develop ourselves in a particular way, we are nevertheless involved in a martial art that presupposes working with a partner. Doing a solo form gives us an opportunity to concentrate on and to perfect the movements we might use if an opponent were actually present.

Another aspect of the individual form is its suitability for meditation. As they do the form, students learn to focus their minds as fully as possible from moment to moment on the form's changing patterns. Obviously, thoughts unrelated to tai chi will intrude, but if a thought is not held or embraced, it will depart. Unfortunately, for those who hoped the problem would end there, the departing thought will be replaced by a new one clamoring for attention. Focusing on the form will weaken the intensity of extraneous thoughts and help to teach us to concentrate. This kind of practice, if done over time with no attachment to results, has the ability to calm and settle us. It can open our minds to an increased appreciation for the richness and diversity of the world around us and a better sense of our connection with it all. In short, the many benefits claimed for meditation can accrue to us as we practice the individual form.

To elaborate a bit more on the tai chi form's meditative quality, Chinese masters have over the centuries spoken of the *chi* and of the need to allow it to sink to the *tan t'ien*. The mainstream Western scientific establishment regards concepts centering around chi as vague and, in fact, thinks many of the ideas and practices of Chinese medicine not far from superstition. Yet those of us with firsthand experience of Chinese medicine know that it can help us heal if we are ill just as Western medicine can and sometimes with far fewer harmful side effects. One big difference between the two systems is that the Chinese explanation of the functioning of the body often has to do with processes that may not depend only on the physical presence of organs or on passageways physiologically discernible. Moreover, because Chinese thinking springs from a linguistic base different from the Indo-European, their way of seeing the world will differ from ours in the West. On this subject, it is quite interesting that more than fifty years ago Benjamin Lee Whorf made a study of American Indian languages and found himself in a world alien to speakers of Indo-European languages. His work brought him to the theory that " . . . every language is a vast pattern-system, different from others, in which are culturally ordained the forms and categories by which the personality not only communicates, but also analyzes nature, notices or neglects types of relationship and phenomena, channels his reasoning, and builds the house of his consciousness." (Whorf, Benjamin Lee, *Language, Thought and Reality,* John

B. Carroll, ed., M.I.T. Press, Cambridge, Mass., 1956, p. 252.)

Whatever the explanation for it, when tai chi masters speak of chi going to the tan t'ien, they mean more than energy gathering in the lower abdomen. They believe that a settling and centering gradually occur in our body as we practice. Images of the Buddha often show him with a huge belly, but perhaps to the disappointment of those whose tendencies go in this direction, bringing chi to the tan t'ien does not require gaining weight. Rather, the belief of the Japanese and Chinese is that if one's energy goes to this lower center one thinks and feels in a grounded, more settled way. This grounding puts us more in tune with the earth. They contrast this with our Western generally more cerebral approach to life, characterized by our body's higher center. An extreme example of an overly cerebral way of thinking is sometimes portrayed in sketches of a mad professor who, with seeming scientific reasonableness, conceives destructive plans for some part of the world. In its less extreme form it can lead to overdoing in ways that at first glance might seem logical and even beneficial, but which ignore or rationalize away possible adverse effects, especially those that might only become apparent some years in the future.

Meditative training like tai chi chuan can, then, act to quiet and deemphasize the analytical, logically reasoning manner that our culture believes is the correct way to order and process the chaos of the world. Such a deemphasis might allow more play to our mind's intuitive functioning. There is nothing wrong with, and much to be gained by, using our mind analytically, but to use it almost exclusively in this way is unbalanced and has a not insignificant responsibility for the perilous state of affairs on our planet. Though the odds against it happening seem to be mounting, perhaps a more intuitive way of thinking about the world might help us to recognize and reduce in time our overdevelopment of and overdependence on the ever-growing machinery that is supposed to make our lives easier and better. We are swept along by technological development so that in our urban environment, many of us interact increasingly with electronic devices and less with other human beings. In addition, our culture is gradually losing our knowledge of and our direct connection with the natural or unprocessed things of the earth. With a more intuitive way of thinking about our lives could come the realization that our very survival may depend on the other forms of life our present political and economic systems are destroying. At the least, a better synthesis than we have now between the analytical and the intuitive, in which the intuitive gets equal attention, seems necessary to our longer-term welfare.

Another useful product of learning the tai chi form is its introduction of discipline into our daily routine. We will probably not do push-hands every day, because arranging for a partner with whom to practice is not always easy, yet we can and should do the form daily. But our sense of discipline should not be the only factor keeping us to a regular practice routine, because the form must attract us and be enjoyable if we are to continue with it. Nevertheless, we will encounter many days when we will not feel like doing it and our progress in tai chi will be slower if we fail to do the form even on those days when our enthusiasm or energy levels are low. I have found that the discipline developed in one area of life can often carry over into other areas. In the case of the closely related tai chi form and push-hands, the disciplined approach to practice characteristic of form training will help us in our efforts at learning push-hands. Keeping at something even though we experience discouragement and frustration is of great value.

Even those whose main interest in tai chi chuan may be in doing push-hands will clearly benefit by learning the solo form. In almost all cases there is little choice in the matter, because learning the form before pushing hands is the preferred sequence in tai chi chuan. After students have learned the form and have begun push-hands some of them may give the form little attention, practicing it only sporadically. This decision is unfortunate because the form and push-hands compliment each other; what we learn in the form helps our pushing and our pushing helps our form. Another problem along these lines occurs in the reverse way where students may like doing the individual form, but despite their teacher's urging balk at continuing their training when it involves an opponent. This is also an obviously misguided notion, probably rising from our generally short-term approach to activities we pursue and from our individualistic attitude that may make it difficult for us to accept a teacher's guidance.

A final word concerning the relationship between the tai chi form and push-hands is that the transition from learning and doing the form to learning push-hands goes more smoothly and easily when we teach push-hands in a noncompetitive way. Ideally, we can maintain the same mental attitude in push-hands that we hold when we do the solo form. That is, we should try to adhere to Taoist principles whether or not we are faced with an opponent.

Before learning tai chi chuan, I studied and taught judo and karate and gained some familiarity with aikido. I always found engaging in contests unpleasantly stressful, though I did well in the many tournaments I entered. Over the years, however, I became convinced that taking part in contests and developing the way of thinking that sees others and other manifestations of the world around us as entities to be conquered or overcome is not good for us or for whatever we interact with. I have attempted in some of the following chapters to set down the reasons for my thinking about competition as I do, and for recommending training in push-hands along lines that downplay the competitive aspect.

I have been a teacher of various martial arts since 1952. I began teaching judo at a rather early age, because the United States in the fifties had developed relatively few judo instructors so that even a person with the lowly rank of *shodan* (first degree black belt) could readily find students eager to learn. Judo was advertised and understood to be a method by which a smaller, weaker person could throw or subdue a larger, stronger one. The secret supposedly lay in using an opponent's strength to defeat him. Because karate had not yet been at all widely introduced to the U. S., the general public thought the judo of the late '40s and early '50s included striking techniques and self-defense moves. While it is true that judo includes such techniques, they were usually taught only to high-ranking black belts. The judo usually taught at a judo school or club was the throwing and mat work of sport judo. These techniques were easily adaptable to self-defense but this was not the emphasis.

Judo as a system was started in the 1880s in Japan by Kano, Jigoro. He envisioned it as mental and physical training for everyone: men, women, young, and old. Promotion to higher rank in judo came through testing in grading contests with no weight classes that were held once or twice a year.

Over the decades, however, judo became more sportive and the leadership organized many more contests. After World War II, as judo spread more widely throughout the world, the heads of judo in Japan, partly in the belief that Japan could dominate this activity, strongly supported international competition. In 1953, reflecting this growing interest in judo and the organizational talents of ranked judo players and teachers, the U. S. held its first judo nationals, an annual event thereafter.

When it came to be considered mainly as a sport, judo's character changed in emphasis and intensity. My own sense of it as I began judo practice during the last years of the forties was that winning was much more desirable than losing and that physical strength played an important part in achieving superiority over an opponent. It was not that I used only strength to win my matches, because I gave technique adequate attention, but that I performed the pulling and off-balancing part of my throws more powerfully than opponents anticipated. At the time I also practiced hand balancing, gymnastics, and weight lifting, supplementary activities that helped my coordination and strength. At any rate, my emphasis in sport judo was not on refined and perhaps exquisite sensitivity and technique, but on strength, speed, and whatever attributes I could bring to bear, short of illegal tactics, to overcome my opponents. My approach enabled me to win almost all my matches and earned the respect of most people engaged or interested in judo. I attributed churlishness and ethnocentricism to individuals who seemed less taken with my achievements than I thought warranted. It did not occur to me that I might be going in the wrong direction, if my aim in martial arts training was to gain a better understanding of the nature of things (or however we express an attempt to grasp what life is about).

Thus, the evolution of judo, or at least its change over the decades to an increasingly sportive or competitive endeavor, seemed to be accompanied by a growing belief among judo players that judo was about winning matches. (This was also my initial impression of it, but mine was based on the limited experience and judgment of a nineteen-year-old.) Methods of training and practicing changed and the full range of possibilities judo offered narrowed. Coaches and players introduced strength exercises (lifting weights) and other supplementary additions to training instead of spending that time on the art itself. Players no longer focused primarily on seeking self-perfection nor did they consider important such concepts as subject-object oneness or the interconnectedness of all that exists. These philosophical ideas were not completely dead, were voiced at times by some who believed in them, but were given only lip service by the great majority of judo players. Given the high degree of intensity brought about by our desire to triumph, we usually considered an opponent mainly as someone to defeat. The concepts of oneness with an opponent or of a compassionate regard for an opponent's welfare, were not important to us, if they came into our thoughts at all.

The development of the sport karate we know shares many similarities with judo. But karate, at least that system developed on Okinawa and brought to Japan, might be said to have had a somewhat more utilitarian grounding than did judo. Some few hundred years ago when a ruling Japanese lord forbade Okinawans to own swords, they invented a fighting system that made use of farming implements and hardened surfaces of hands and feet to take the place of the banned swords. Yet karate, too, before it moved into the realm of sport was sometimes taught as an art of self-development and was not to be lightly brought into play.

In its sportive aspect, karate at first went beyond the traditional set attack-response method of practicing with a partner to a more freewheeling freestyle sparring. Blows and kicks were, however, stopped just short of contact and points were awarded on the basis of effective techniques, ones which had they landed on the target would have incapacitated the opponent. For some teachers and systems, however, this method was not realistic enough. Full contact matches, both with protective gloves and footwear and without, began to appear. Of course, certain targets on the body like eyes, throat, and genitals were off-limits to an attack.

Again, clearly, the mind-set necessary for success in sportive, especially full contact, karate tends to differ from that involved in karate training designed for self-development, and seems to hark back to an earlier time when men learned karate for fighting and killing. In the kind of sport karate where the object is to incapacitate the opponent, to knock him down and out, what happens to respect, caring, and identification with one's opponent? Training methods, naturally, reflect the ends that fighters seek. Thus, they practice those techniques that will win matches, usually to the exclusion of the development of a more rounded repertoire. Teachers and students downplay or ignore the possibility that the art is concerned with mental and spiritual development, and training is conducted as if considerations other than winning matches did not exist.

Tai chi chuan in its push-hands aspect also seems in the U. S. to be moving toward sportiveness. It is true that in China students from schools of tai chi chuan enter and win "any style" contests in which blows and kicks are exchanged and the survivor goes on to the next match. It is again obvious that preparing for such contests calls for appropriate training. Under these conditions, the Taoist philosophical principles underlying tai chi chuan might well receive rather short shrift.

My concern is, however, not with tai chi in China, but with the direction of tai chi in the West and, more specifically, the U. S. I believe we err in attempting to make tai chi more sportive. Tai chi offers us an opportunity to relax, to open up, to ground and center ourselves. Doing the individual tai chi form is useful in achieving these results, but I believe push-hands plays an even more important role. Yet, for push-hands to change students' ways of thinking and acting, it must be performed over some years according to strict tai chi principles. If this condition is not met, students will not develop in the way that tai chi masters say is possible. Students who are attracted to competitive push-hands will develop some level of skill in avoiding and resisting pushes, and in pushing, but they will fail woefully in achieving the much more important and valuable changes in themselves push-hands could make possible.

I will discuss push-hands and its potential for development in greater detail in a later chapter. But it may be useful to our understanding of this subject to ask at the outset why many students interested in self-development or self-realization fail to follow tai chi principles when they begin practicing with an opponent and are drawn instead toward resisting pushes and to using strength. A few answers come quickly to mind. First, it seems to take too long using tai chi principles to get results, if by "results" we mean to push our opponent or avoid being pushed. Imagining we see little improvement in our pushing after a year or two of practice, and little change in ourselves despite our daily form practice, many of us think we are unsuited to this kind of training or that we have little hope of "getting it." If we continue we may decide to forget or to deemphasize tai chi principles and self-realization, and begin using strength, especially if we can dominate our opponents or, at least, hold our own through this method. Second, push-hands done according to tai chi principles is alien to us, to the way we conduct ourselves in daily life. That is, invariably if we are pushed we resist. If our own attempt to push meets resistance, we push harder. But these seemingly natural and reflexive actions can be changed, as can our perspective on things and the way we view the world. Unfortunately for those who hope for results in these areas, changing our conditioned reflexes and our way of seeing is a matter of many years' training. One big difficulty in making such changes through push-hands is that we tend to push in the way we live our daily lives. To see more clearly, ultimately, we must break the hold on our minds of our acculturation. But without strict attention to this new tai chi way of interacting, and strict adherence to the principles involved, we will adjust and manipulate this potentially valuable, but alien, training method until it fits comfortably into our individualistic and competitive culture.

II.
The Competitive Milieu

HOW DOES OUR CULTURE teach us to see and to deal with the world around us? Our society seems a highly competitive one. Even as little children our parents and teachers compare our progress or development with that of other children in all kinds of areas, ranging from physical growth to intelligence. These constant comparisons with others, or measurement against some standard, can serve to form our thinking about ourselves into unhealthy patterns. If we are preoccupied with evaluation, no matter where we fall on a particular scale we can experience problems with our idea of ourselves. Stated simply, if we fall too low on some scale we might feel inferior and suffer from low self-esteem. If we score high we may have an inflated view of our abilities and become arrogant. No matter where we fall on some measurement scale, if we take evaluation too seriously, we might well find some reason to react in some negative way.

From a slightly different standpoint, when we compare ourselves with others in some area we can almost always find someone who is doing less well than we. On the other hand, we can also discover some who seem to surpass us. Attaching importance to either comparison is detrimental to a well-balanced state of mind. Moreover, making such comparisons is a waste of energy as well as a misdirection of focus from the correct one of doing the best we can with the resources we have.

If we judge our standing in any area of life by a comparison with others, we will find incomprehensible such a concept as "just be." The ideas that usually we are all right as we are, that we are where we need to be and doing what we need to be doing to further our particular level of development will seem strange. Of course, the overly simple formulas for living we often read about will not be enough to support us in the difficult situations all of us will meet sometime in our life. Fortunately, methods other than intellectual concepts or simple formulas are available to help us to cope and one of these will be considered in a later chapter. It seems clear, however, that our society's tendency to compare us with one another and to measure individuals on some scale serves to pit us against others and to introduce, encourage, and emphasize our separateness from one another. This emphasis on comparison does little to promote our well-being in the sense of our feeling content with our level of ability and achievement.

Another example of our culture's preoccupation with comparison and quantification appears in our attitude toward sports. Few of us actually play a sport on an ongoing basis. We may blame the system, saying that we lack the skill to be chosen for a team or can't find the time to practice. We are a nation of sports watchers rather than players. Following the progress of a favorite team has great appeal, judging by the attention devoted to sports in the news media. But although we may enjoy watching highly talented and accomplished professional athletes in action, to witness their timing, concentration, and fluid movement, such aspects of the game seem of less concern to us than whether our favorite team won or lost. Learning the final scores of contests or games is usually uppermost in our minds when we check the sports page. A hard-fought game may end with one team defeating the other by only a narrow margin, but we think of the defeated team as somehow of inferior stuff compared with the winner, even though the teams may differ little in terms of ability or desire. Though we may be impressed by outstanding individual performances, even those by members of the losing team, our way of judging a team's performance is ultimately by the final score. We know that losers fail to make the playoffs or are otherwise eliminated from contending further and we are used to the process of making easily quantifiable comparisons.

In track and field events, the difference between the first few places among top competitors often can be measured in very small increments of a few hundredths of a second. Yet, when we evaluate these athletes' performance we do so on the basis of these small differences instead of in some way that recognizes the beauty of the athletes' physical movement or interaction with their environment. Most would argue that this clocking method of determining the top performers is perfectly logical and valid and, given the need to have a winner in a race, I would have to agree. But if we think that determining winners is of less importance than is the actual participation of the players in an athletic event or game, we must approach contests in a different frame of mind than we do now. However, changing our approach to one aspect of our culture is difficult, because cultures are internally fairly consistent. A basic shift in the way we view all of life is necessary if our attitude toward any particular area, such as sports, were to change.

An even more striking indicator than sports of our basic beliefs about life is our behavior in the workplace. Perhaps our sense that life is competition stems from our experience with the working world of our society. In an economic system based on the operation of the marketplace, managers compare their results with that of other companies and are keenly aware of how their product is selling and of whether other companies are in any sense outdoing their own. If a company seems to be falling behind in productivity or profitability, its managers may reduce the work force, replace nonproductive workers, or at least urge everyone to work harder. To heighten efficiency, they may attempt to upgrade the many physical aspects of their operation. If one company makes a significant breakthrough in some part of its manufacturing process, rival companies will make every effort to learn its secret, even resorting to illegal means such as industrial espionage. Because they see the world in this way and because they may derive some advantage from it, industry leaders may describe their industry as in a life or death struggle with its counterpart in foreign countries.

Under these conditions, and given the often distorted spin on events provided by politicians and the media in their effort to describe and to influence what is going on, the individual worker cannot but feel that competition is the way the real world operates and is natural. Also, on a personal level, workers are well attuned to the idea that they must compete with other candidates for an entry position in some company and that their progress once they are hired will often depend on outdoing their rivals. Workers may notice also that multinational companies avail themselves of cheaper labor and more favorable conditions in countries other than the one considered their home, giving rise to the thought that the welfare of workers at home is of secondary importance after company profitability.

Despite the foregoing strong evidence that the world is competitive, with all that implies for individual and group behavior, we should not close our mind to the possibility that the picture is somehow distorted. Perhaps we are seeing things incorrectly when we believe competition predominates in individual and world affairs. Some have said that life is much more cooperative than competitive and that if uncontrolled competition were the rule, life on our planet could hardly survive. For instance, on an individual and personal level the various components of our body combine and cooperate to keep us healthy and functioning. Ill health results if our various organs fail to regulate their functioning in correct relation to one another or if cells suddenly proliferate without regard to the rest of the organism. Another example of cooperative endeavor is the giving up of individualistic striving in favor of working as part of a team. Other cooperative elements in our world are discernible in such a phenomenon as individual workers combining to form unions to try to strengthen their bargaining power with management. On another level, management may attempt to align its company with other companies to increase pressure on the government to force or fashion a more favorable governmental policy toward their industry. In some countries governmental agencies work together with industry to adjust policy so that it is conducive to the country's optimum economic growth. Thus, if we are open to seeing it, there is certainly evidence that the elements that make up our world, from the smallest to the largest, work more rather than less cooperatively. This realization should give us a strong hint that pursuing an essentially cooperative course in our lives may be of more benefit than following a competitive one.

In this vein, the work on management technique of W. Edwards Deming might prove instructive. The Japanese have accorded Deming high honors for introducing them to his theories on how companies can operate to produce a better and cheaper product. The salient features of his advice are that all the divisions of a company are equally important, everyone in the company should be heard, and that all workers should attempt unceasingly to improve whatever they are doing. This results not in a joyless, competitive atmosphere, but in a cooperative one in which everyone can benefit. The game is not a zero-sum one in which there are winners and losers. Instead, because the quality of the end product becomes ever higher and the cost lower, everyone involved wins.

Deming maintains that to institute such a system people's thinking must change and that the process takes years, if not decades, to show notable results. Aware of the Japanese success in world trade, some U. S. companies and government agencies, the U. S. Navy prominently among them, have been putting Deming's theories into practice. In manufacturing processes where quality rather than quantity is of first importance, Deming's ideas seem to produce superior results. His theories concerning how people can work together cooperatively and more productively through valuing each person's contribution to the final product are valid not only for manufacturing firms but for all kinds of human enterprise.

Nevertheless, in the U. S., though the thinking may be mistaken, the pervading atmosphere in the world of work is competitive, where workers often feel they must vie with one another for advancement and believe management tries to exploit them to increase profits. Here company directors distrust and resent government and its attempt to regulate industrial growth, and use the threat of foreign domination of world markets to justify often unwelcome labor practices. Because it may well be that a competitive environment reduces rather than increases our satisfaction with our lives, in the next chapter we will further discuss competition to try to determine its positive and negative aspects.

III.

Positive and Negative Aspects of Competition

OUR BELIEF THAT THE real world is a competitive one may be reinforced not only by those aspects of our lives discussed in the previous chapter but by various seemingly beneficial or useful effects of competition. For example, in sports the attempt by athletes to outdo one another has over the years continued to improve standards in every track and field event. Better equipment and better training methods have played a role in raising standards, but these developments can also be considered products of competition.

The spur of competing against others might take us beyond the limits we imagine confine us, making us try harder and helping us exceed our earlier best. Before a runner broke the four-minute-mile barrier runners believed humans were physically incapable of running the mile this quickly. But when someone demonstrated the possibility, others soon also reduced their time below four minutes. However, breaking four minutes in the mile run might have been made possible for runners as much by a changed mental outlook as by an attempt to surpass a rival's performance, of a determination not to be left behind or any other competitive rationale or motive. No doubt, any number of reasons or combination of them may be responsible for an athlete's performance level, but it is quite possible that a competitive drive need not be foremost among them.

Furthermore, in some areas of life competition may not play much of a part in improving performance. For example, I have heard music commentators say that Beethoven's expression of the human experience of life through the music he wrote has never been surpassed. Art as well as most other human endeavors builds on what has gone before, but an individual through his particular genius and application may do something that no one could do before or since. The factors that make possible such an accomplishment probably depend little on competitive motivation.

Another example of an unparalleled achievement occurred in the construction of stringed instruments by Stradivarius. Violin makers have been trying since his death to duplicate his work but without success. Craftsmen have selected the right kind of wood, shaped and measured as accurately as possible, used computers wherever these machines could provide additional help—all in vain. The tone was always inferior to the originals. Some have said that it was the varnish Stradivarius used that made the difference, because we have been unable to come up with the same, or the right, formula. The competitive drive may have spurred Stradivarius on, we don't know this for certain, but it was not enough, if it was in operation, to allow the craftsmen who followed him to equal, let alone surpass him.

Although violin makers continue to make instruments and the foregoing instance concerns the issue of quality, we may notice, also, that some arts flower, continue to grow for a time, go into decline, and finally are lost. The role of competition in this rise and fall would be very difficult to establish.

Returning to sports, it is clear that successfully competing brings financial rewards, sometimes seemingly out of proportion to the effort expended. In addition, competitors' egos are stroked as fans gather around winners perhaps hoping to absorb some of whatever it is that makes them win or, at the least, sharing in the temporary euphoria of the winning effort. To win seems, then, to competitors and spectators alike far preferable to losing, even if they are not satisfying a personal competitive drive.

Turning to the business world, the competition between companies on both the domestic and international scene could be thought responsible for breakthroughs in technology and production methods that have led to economic gains. Such gains doubtless have improved the material life and raised living standards in the countries where the companies are located.

The situation is hardly, however, so straightforward. Improvement in a country's economy depends on far more than any form the competitive element may assume. The economic environment, for example, must be conducive to free trade. Protectionism in trade or more open antagonism between nations stifle trade and produce stagnant national economies. Countries with superior military technology and forces have used their power to control production and the economy in weaker nations to the detriment of workers in the weaker countries. In modern times stronger nations have used weaker ones as sources of raw materials and as markets for the output of the stronger's industries. Workers in the subjugated or controlled nations do not thrive under these conditions, no matter the degree of their competitive drive.

Defenders of colonialism argue that a world in which a stronger, more vibrant country controls a weaker one is properly ordered. They cite, among other reasons, the greater energy, industriousness, and inventiveness of the people in the controlling nation as reasons for their domination of the weaker nation. Darwinian theory applied to nation states has been used to bolster this argument. "Survival of the fittest" is taken to mean that it is natural, or the way the world works, to have those nations that can best adapt to their environment emerge victorious over the less adaptive.

Warfare might be seen as a clear example of one country overcoming another in the drive for dominance and influence in the world. Yet we cannot but have reservations about this proposition as we follow the course of events in the twentieth century that led to the U. S. position as the only remaining superpower. The peace settlements following World War I would seem to have rewarded the victors in that war and established their hegemony over the losers. But in the short span of twenty years in Europe, Germany reemerged as a major threat to the new order. In Asia, Japan although not an Allied enemy in World War I, entertained visions in the 1920s and '30s of playing the leading role, to the exclusion or weakening of western influence. The U. S. and its allies met and successfully overcame these attempts to reduce their power and influence in the world through a costly World War II. Peace treaties following the war, again, seemed to reward the victorious nations. But new problems quickly emerged in the form of a hostile Soviet Union, and in the attempt of former colonial nations to assume and fight for self-rule. These negative (from our standpoint) developments, especially in former colonial nations, might well have been precipitated or accelerated by the upheavals and opportunities afforded by World War II. Before long it seemed expedient for the U. S. to help Germany and Japan back to productivity and some degree of economic power as a counter to the newly perceived threats posed by the Soviet Union.

As the years went by and we struggled to maintain the world order mandated by our political and economic theories and beliefs, events made clear that our power to control the rest of the world was declining. For example, our Vietnam experience demonstrated the limits of our military power, as well as brought into question the basic tenets of our foreign policy. In addition, the growing economic strength of our former enemies, Germany and Japan, revealed flaws and weaknesses in our industrial capabilities and, ultimately, economic power.

Moreover, as a side issue in our attempt to dominate our potential enemies or rivals, we developed and, through intentional and unintentional means, spread weapons of mass destruction throughout the world. Although these cataclysmic weapons might be considered to have been responsible for maintaining a standoff and avoiding a major war over the past four or five decades, their potential for the destruction of our modern civilization had and continues to have a strong negative effect on our psychological health.

Our "defense" efforts and our attempt through the exercise of military and economic power to maintain a stable world under our control have cost us vast amounts of resources. This loss of wealth is not without precedent because some economists maintain that the Pax Brittanica, established and maintained by Great Britain for about one hundred years throughout most of the nineteenth and into the twentieth centuries, finally became too costly and was one of the major factors in undermining Britain's influence in the world.

Winning a war, then, does not seem to confer the benefits on the victor that one might expect. Anticipated benefits might be enjoyed by the winner for a time, but in our rapidly changing world additional, usually unexpected, variables may work to undermine a superior position, making the enjoyment of the gains of warfare of relatively short duration. In fact, we have seen militarily vanquished enemy nations assuming positions in the world through economic means, which they were unsuccessful in achieving through warfare.

Perhaps the warfare of ancient times gave more clear-cut victories and losses than is true of the past century. If a state fell to a stronger foe, historians tell us that all males might have been put to death and the women enslaved. The winner would then become richer through adding the spoils of war to the national treasure and would be able to exercise dominion over the conquered land. The question of competition under such harsh conditions, however, where survival itself is of paramount importance, seems of minor relevance.

Approaching the subject of competition from a slightly different angle, it is an oversimplification to view nations as large human beings, attributing to their actions the thinking, feeling, and motivation of the individual person. Nevertheless, we find it convenient to speak of a national character, the way people in a society generally view life and conduct themselves, despite the fact that particular individuals in that society will differ radically both from one another and from the generally accepted model. But the mix of ideas and attitudes shared by the majority in a society will go a long way toward forming the character of most of the individuals who comprise it. Thus, despite inconsistencies and ongoing change, each society will be something of an interlocked, all of a piece, kind of organism. In America, our strong individualism, competitive drive, cavalier attitude toward the earth and its creatures, and the paternalistic nature of our religious beliefs all shape and are shaped by us. It is no surprise that ours is a highly litigious society with an inordinate number of lawyers, compared with other developed countries, who make it their business to protect everyone's "rights." Our way of behaving toward one another and of settling our quarrels is estimated to cost our industry additional billions that all of us ultimately must pay in the form of higher prices for goods. The costs we pay in other ways may be even greater when we consider that the factors that form Americans may make us both contentious and unwilling in disputes to enlist and abide by the ruling of a third-party mediator. In addition, we are not averse to the use of violence to right perceived wrongs. All of these elements reinforce our sense of separateness from one another and, ultimately, increase our feelings of loneliness.

Of course, we should not forget that Americans possess qualities, like our character traits of openness, frankness, and kindliness, which many in the world find admirable. They also comment favorably on our energy, pragmatism, and ability to get things done. Nevertheless, America is probably the foremost representative of that Western combination of Judeo-Christian and Greco-Roman thinking about and attitude toward nature and the world, especially the subjugation of everything around him to man's will, which underlies the rise of Western science and the accompanying development of technology. The West has been able to dominate and to spread its influence throughout the rest of the world through the power of its scientific achievements and their extension into politics and economics. But our Western way of interacting with the world has, for many reasons, increasingly become a disharmonious one, as compared with groups such as the North Americans (before Europeans arrived) or the Bedouins who were able to live for thousands of years without destroying or exhausting the environment that nourished them. At any rate, it seems undeniable that the West, and Western thinking, bears much of the responsibility for the dangerous condition of today's world.

If we are to alter the disastrous course we seem embarked upon, it could well be that our thinking and the very way we see the world have to change. A basic change in our outlook could, without addressing the issue directly, deemphasize competitiveness in our dealings with one another and in the negotiations of our leaders with the leaders of other nations. We might think that even without a changed outlook reason alone would dictate and inspire the use of greater cooperativeness in world affairs based on the concept of the "global village" and the need to fashion agreements limiting the possibilities for unrestrained action by individuals or countries. In recent years nations have actually moved toward an ever larger measure of national and international control and cooperation as they have become aware of environmental or other threats to their welfare and tried to act to contain or avert impending dangers.

But others would argue that the impress of acculturation is too strong and that we and our leaders are locked into certain mind-sets by our training, by our beliefs about reality, and by the structure of our language. Perhaps the danger of the collapse of our present civilization will provide the impetus necessary for developing different thinking about and approaches to our problems.

In sum, even a cursory examination of the world history of the twentieth century reveals that past problems were much more complicated and included far more variables than could be settled or handled by an overriding concern for emerging the victor in a competition. Those who favor competition and believe we must prepare ourselves to compete successfully are oversimplifying the majority of issues of concern in our time. Far more important is the question of how we can effect a basic change in the way we see and relate to the world. This seems essential if we are to avoid the suffering our present direction makes likely. A radical shift in outlook would probably make of minor relevance such an issue as competition. Instead of merely having as our goal the defeat of an adversary, we might, with the underlying understanding that all life is connected and that our adversary's victories and defeats are ours as well, attempt to be moderate in the benefits we seek, try to avoid extremes, and make appropriate moves in a timely and restrained way. This pattern of behavior is, not coincidentally, similar to what we learn to do in tai chi chuan.

Many would argue that such thinking and behavior would end in defeat at the hands of a ruthless adversary who might not play by the rules or by one who is much stronger or more skillful than we. Of course, if we are unevenly matched, a more vigorous attack and defense would probably have no more chance of success than the recommended one. In the case of an adversary whose demands are to us clearly unreasonable and who does not wish to cooperate in striking a mutually agreeable bargain, we could do worse than to follow the restrained, middle way of continuing to attempt to come to a mutually beneficial agreement.

We should be aware, also, that making careful and measured replies and demonstrating willingness to yield on some points in a dispute is not a total giving up of our position. We must attempt tenaciously to attain our ends (moderate though they may be) and our means must be in accord with the restrained approach expressed earlier. An example of a seemingly ineffective method eventually triumphing over superior force is

Gandhi's use of *satyagraha* (nonviolence or passive resistance) in India to achieve his political and social goals.

Remember, too, that the preliminary aspects of an impending clash are just as, if not more, important than the final confrontation. A person who has developed the ability to see the world differently usually possesses a mind that has opened enough to entertain more than one way of dealing with a problem. Such a person might well happen upon or creatively fashion a satisfactory solution to a problem that could avoid a final confrontation, especially when an adversary's forces are superior and, on the present course, defeat seems assured. At any rate, it is hoped that the suggested method of dealing with adversaries will both satisfy our desire to integrate with the rhythms of the world and be flexible and adaptable enough to allow us to perform creditably in any situation.

IV.

The Difficulty of Changing Thinking and Behavior

AS THE LAST CHAPTER SUGGESTS, a great deal has been written about the disasters awaiting us in a relatively short time if we fail to change the way we live. We read that if we do nothing about the population explosion and the deteriorating environment, we seem headed for a world where hundreds of millions will starve and where the quality of life even for those with enough food will appreciably diminish. Negative forces, which cannot easily be halted or redirected, have already been set in motion. For example, air pollution is a condition apparently responsible for a marked increase in people's respiratory ills, for the acid rain that is poisoning our land and water, and for a possible increase in global temperatures. Will industrial nations cut back production or install equipment in their factories at great expense to reduce harmful emissions? A nation unilaterally taking this course would face economic ruin. The citizens of democratic societies in which government decided to clean up the environment at tremendous cost would quickly vote out of office those responsible for the consequent decline in their living standard.

Though politicians may attempt to take a longer view and call for sacrifice for the sake of future generations, the realities of a democratic system of government and a capitalistic economic system militate against such a course. The past few decades are clear witness to how slowly world leaders, no matter their system of government, have responded to environmental threats and how short a period of time they have taken into account when planning for the future. In our own country, preparing now for conditions that we might face in twenty-five years seems to the electorate premature and unnecessary, especially if such preparation entails cutting back on the wasteful style of life we think is our due and have come to take for granted. Nor is there clear consensus among the many experts who make pronouncements about such possibilities as global warming or the disappearance of additional portions of the ozone layer. Those with a vested interest in continuing economic practices probably harmful to our well-being can usually find some reputable scientists who disagree with the warnings of most of their scientific peers. Their contrary view may differ markedly from the thesis most scientists support or when they do agree they may disagree with the timing. Malthusian warnings on population growth outstripping the food supply seem logically well founded, but the timing of the catastrophe is uncertain, because our ability to grow more food has continued to increase.

A related point is that many people believe that human ingenuity and intelligence will solve the problems caused by our increasing population, repair ecological damage, and produce for those of us in the developed countries, and perhaps even for the whole world, an ever better living standard. Those who are in this camp point to past beneficial technological achievements as evidence that we have always come up with generally agreeable solutions to our problems. They ignore arguments which hold that the problems facing us are of a magnitude far greater than any we have faced in the past and that we are fast depleting and poisoning the basic resources that might give us the time and the opportunity to regroup and to correct earlier mistakes. Alternatives to getting our raw material from earth, like mining other planets and shipping these products to earth, or gene splicing to synthesize substitutes for oil and other raw materials, seem unworkable in a practical way in the foreseeable future, if at all.

Therefore, unless our way of thinking changes, and by this I mean how we feel about and relate to one another and to the world around us, it seems doubtful that we will be able to avoid the many disasters predicted by those thinkers pessimistic about our future. Radical change in our circumstances and in our thinking might result from a sudden catastrophe of some sort like one or more devastating earthquakes, volcanic eruptions, or nuclear explosions (Chernobyl or nuclear warfare), any of which could cause crippling infrastructure damage in developed nations, kill and injure great numbers, and interfere with our ability to grow enough food. Of course, an unexpected catastrophe would just more quickly bring about the miserable conditions predicted for the longer term if we continue on our present course. Presented with a sudden world support system collapse we would just have to do our best to cope, having ignored or not received warnings that might have given many of us time to make preparations to survive. As things stand now we seem to have the opportunity to change our way of life and to try to avoid or, at least, to moderate the effects of an impending disaster. Whether or not we will be able to alter our positions in time is a difficult and long question.

Suppose we believe the pessimists who warn us of dire consequences if we continue to abuse our planet as we have been doing. Taoist philosophy tells us to let things alone and cautions against overdoing. But it seems we might be justified in taking some action that may consist of withdrawing from an overextended position. If we are certain that we must do something to change things, how might we proceed?

Given our culture's passionate embrace of cause-and-effect linear thinking, rationality, and the scientific method in almost all areas of human endeavor, we live in an intellectual climate in which few of us dare state our misgivings about the course of future events based on philosophical principles or some kind of intuition. Moreover, if most people in our society doubted a disaster was really in the offing, we would have a difficult time convincing them even if we held a respected position. Without concrete evidence of some impending unpleasantness relatively few would heed our warnings. The average citizen who psychically foresaw a calamity could exert even less influence through such channels as writing letters to congresspeople and to newspapers, or joining like-minded activists.

If, then, warnings to change our ways based on an intuitive sense of impending catastrophe will sway few, perhaps we might have more success if we tried to persuade people to change their thinking and behavior through reasoned argument. By presenting pertinent facts and suggesting the probable consequences of a course of action, we could attempt to alert the public to the folly of continuing present practices. But the great majority, who are by and large committed to their way of living, might well resist our reasoning, viewing our argument as an attack on their lifestyle. Perhaps those looking for some alternative to an overextended and unsatisfying way of life may be attracted to what we have to say. Yet even when people recognize the validity of an argument, their behavior may not accord with this recognition. They will often say one thing and do another. Especially is this so if a contemplated behavior change entails some degree of sacrifice and discomfort.

In the meantime, if we spend a considerable amount of time and energy actively trying to change people's thinking, how are we living our lives? Under these circumstances we tend to neglect, or reduce the care given to, our immediate sphere. Although activists would resist the notion, it is possible that instead of directing our energies to the wider world, we might exert greater influence if we do our best to care for what is closest to hand. At least this is the point from which we should begin. It could be that positive changes in a kind of ripple effect could come about incrementally as people are attracted to not just ideas but to an example of someone's living a life of personally looking after a bit of the world.

V.

Learning to See the World Differently

I T SEEMS EVIDENT THAT changing our thinking and behavior, even when we might admit the necessity for such change, is not easy. In this connection, the reason for the earlier discussion on competition was to make the point that competitive behavior seems a symptom of a failure to see the world clearly, and to alert students and teachers of methods designed to direct people's behavior into more harmonious channels to the inappropriateness of using and encouraging competition to further students' development. More specifically, competition, with its focus on defeating the opponent, runs counter to those objectives of our tai chi training which center around relaxing, letting go and opening up. It simply reinforces the questionable prevailing thinking of our culture about how the world is ordered and operates.

Some might argue that competing in tai chi push-hands or in doing the form will free us of a preoccupation with winning and losing, but my decades of experience with martial arts competition fails to support this argument. I believe thinking and acting competitively will make it more difficult for us to attain the results we may hope for from tai chi chuan. When we find ourselves in a dispute we do not want our reactions to rise from the often ruthless cast of mind our martial arts training, where it is geared to competition or fighting, has instilled in us. Rather, we hope our training will eventually allow us to react with the necessary sensitivity to grasp and interact harmoniously in the situation with whatever elements are involved.

In the final analysis, we are really concerned with the need for training ourselves to be better grounded, in the sense of our awareness of the interconnectedness of everything and, thus, clearer about reality. But in the West we will often believe training is unnecessary and that we will be able to incorporate an attractive world view into our way of behaving because it seems reasonable and appeals to our intellect. Unfortunately, when we attempt to rely on this kind of intellectually apprehended concept in an emergency it often fails us and we soon realize that such concepts take us only a small part of the way to internalizing a world view and to real understanding. Luckily, for those who feel the need to get beyond abstractions to a more concrete base, during the past few thousand years teachers in various cultures have suggested not just the use of language but the practice of nonverbal meditation as a way to sense the rhythms of the world around us and to integrate ourselves with them. They maintain that as we practice daily over the years we will reach understandings and develop in ways that the language of our culture will probably be incapable of expressing.

If we follow this advice, our unfoldment will often move us to live a simpler life and to do without much of the material stuff advertisers tell us will make things easier and us happier. Embarked on this path, we will notice that living more simply with fewer material possessions requires less income. This means that along with other benefits of a less elaborate lifestyle is the possibility of taking a job that is less damaging to our world rather than holding a better paying one the nature of which harms the life support system of future generations.

Our practice may open our minds to the extent that, for example, we find appealing the behavior toward the environment of Native Americans. Most seemed to believe in animism—that everything that springs from the earth possesses a spirit and must be respected and not harmed. Of course, our religious thinkers place animism lower than monotheism on a scale of religious sophistication. But we shouldn't forget that animism helped Native Americans live on their land for thousands of years without exhausting or seriously altering its life-sustaining abilities.

As concerns the issue of competitiveness and the thesis that it is natural for us to compete with one another, the behavior of Indians such as the Hopi refutes this argument. Hopi culture over the past 850 years seems to have emphasized respect for all living things, discouraged competition, and taught its people to live peaceably with other beings and with one another. The fact that a group of human beings has been able to live this way for hundreds of years certainly is a strong indication that behavior is learned and that we are not, by nature, competitive or predatory or whatever label of this nature has been applied to describe us.

We must be careful not to overstate the case, however, or think that the Indians in North America all lived some sort of idyllic life. Their way of life and behavior differed from tribe to tribe, sometimes quite markedly. Their respect for life seems not to have kept some tribes from raiding and killing their neighbors. In some areas population growth outstripped the food supply, causing an advanced society there to suffer a decline and sometimes forcing its members to migrate elsewhere in search of better conditions. Nevertheless, the animistic philosophy that most shared seems to favor the life-sustaining capability of the environment, as contrasted with a philosophy that seeks arrogantly to control nature, holds that everything around us is here primarily for our benefit, and can be used in any way we see fit and, finally, maintains that there need be few limits to ever more growth.

In summary, should we be drawn to the fuller understanding of ourselves and of life seemingly offered by meditation practice, our minds can gradually open to an awareness of the interplay of the forces and rhythms of our world. As mentioned above, such awareness can be the vehicle of sometimes sudden, but more often slow, change in our way of relating to the world and of harmonizing with these forces and rhythms. On this path, in addition to living more simply, we will become less wasteful, desire less, become more conscious of our connection with others and with everything around us, and more solicitous of the welfare of these other forms of life. This list of possibilities for development is not exhaustive nor may everyone who meditates necessarily share all of them. But over the years my students seem to have moved in these directions.

Turning to my own experience of meditative practice, after spending about fifteen years in rather intensive, almost daily martial arts training, I was drawn to the meditative practices of Zen Buddhism. I knew that the basic tenets of Buddhist philosophy underlay the training for living that martial arts provided, and felt that doing *zazen* would strengthen the judo and karate I was teaching, and would further develop my mind and spirit in some salutary way. To pursue this interest I went to Japan to sit for a time at a Zen Buddhist temple. After some months of sitting, however, I felt less than pleased with my zen training and withdrew to spend additional time practicing judo and karate. Another two or three years were to pass before I encountered tai chi chuan, which at the outset I saw as a system of individual form practice and of controlled sparring with a partner, satisfying, to a greater degree than did the judo and karate I had been practicing, my desire for meditation. At the same time, because tai chi chuan was a martial art, and not just meditative training, my connection with these arts remained intact. My tai chi practice slowly brought me to the realization that the more external martial arts I taught, possibly done in a mindful way, could serve as meditative practice to a far greater degree than I had thought possible. However, for a number of reasons, tai chi chuan seemed more suited than the harder martial arts to the kind of training I envisioned would be most beneficial for my students.

To attempt to understand and appreciate the usefulness to our well-being of tai chi chuan, let us examine it in greater detail. As described in the *Tai Chi Handbook,* the tai chi form consists of a sequential series of rhythmic movements performed slowly and varying in length, depending on the style, from seven to over twenty minutes. It is often taught on a superficial level as a mild form of relaxation exercise that can help concentration, strengthen the legs, and reduce mental stress. Most teachers of the form speak of a kind of energy they term *chi*, which circulates in nature and throughout the body along pathways, or meridians. Acupuncturists learn to adjust this flow of energy as necessary to restore balance to our system and to help us heal ourselves. In tai chi form practice we are encouraged to imagine ourselves not only relaxing but allowing these meridians to open so that chi can flow unimpeded, nourish our internal organs, and keep us healthy.

Those teachers with a background in tai chi weapons training will include some edged weapons, especially the sword, in their tai chi instruction. Here the weapon is considered an extension of the hand and of the body. The principles of movement observed in doing the form without a weapon, such as moving from the *tan t'ien* (the body's center), staying relaxed, keeping a low center of gravity, among others, are followed as well in weapons training.

Tai chi masters who teach on a more sophisticated level are knowledgeable about and try to impart the potential of the form as meditative training. As students slowly do the form, they are urged to attempt to concentrate their mind on the gradual change of body, hands, and feet from one position to another, and perhaps on the flow of chi in their body. When an extraneous thought intrudes and clamors for attention, students try to maintain concentration and avoid getting caught.

Some teachers will teach push-hands as well as the form. In push-hands, opponents face each other, and using the very minimum of strength, attempt to disturb each other's balance. To avoid being pushed without resorting to resistance, we have to move our body out of the way of the opponent's attack. We can do this by moving our feet and stepping away or, in the way I favor, by maintaining our foot position and neutralizing the attack by a timely shift of our body.

While it seems fairly evident that doing the solo tai chi form can serve as meditative practice, many are surprised to learn that push-hands is just as, if not more, helpful in allowing us to realize ourselves on levels ranging from the physical to the spiritual. Ideally a tai chi student will train using both the solo form and push-hands. Perhaps because of my years of training in other martial arts, I am strongly attracted to push-hands and in this and in the following chapters have tried to point up the value of push-hands, describe its mechanics, and address the problems most students encounter in their attempt to do this exercise. Let me first mention my particular prejudices, or leanings, in push-hands. It can be taught in a number of ways, ranging from a very soft give-and-take between opponents to an exchange that resembles sumo wrestling. In the very soft style there may be little attempt to break an opponent's balance, the two partners being content to merely "feel each other's energy." The harder approach appeals to those who see push-hands as martial, and who are drawn to competition. I favor a method that falls between these extremes, but what I do has its own rationale and cannot be described simply as a middle road between two extremes. As we proceed this rationale will, I hope, become clear.

Push-hands can teach you to let go of your preconceived ideas about how things are and how the world is. Why is this letting-go valuable? First of all, because we apprehend reality with senses which, even with the aid of our most sophisticated scientific instruments, allow us to grasp only a rather small percentage of the complicated, interlocked, and interdependent elements that make up our world. Thus, as diligent in pursuing knowledge about this world and as intelligent as we may be, our ideas about it will be flawed, incomplete, and probably incorrect.

We do, however, have to make and carry out decisions in our lives and, of course, we base our decisions to a great degree on whatever knowledge we possess. But our decision-making process includes not only the information we can gather about a subject but also our fixed ideas about how the world works and what people are like, ideas that we have somehow picked up from our parents or friends as we grew up or that we formed as a result of past experiences. Many of these ideas, or beliefs, might have served us well in the past, but need to be reexamined and perhaps rejected and replaced by more sophisticated or developed ones, because we have outgrown them or learned to see with greater clarity. For example, "don't cross the street in the middle of the block," "don't talk to strangers" and "mother knows best," were perhaps useful dictums earlier in our lives but need to be reexamined in the light of our maturity. Another example is the categorizing of individuals, the belief that a member of a certain group will embody all of the, usually, negative characteristics of that group. Unfortunately, most of us carry around with us these various preconceived ideas about people, things, and situations. When we are confronted with a crisis that requires action, these ideas usually form a good portion of the basis of our reply.

In push-hands, we see something of this phenomenon in the way we respond to a push. Almost always our body tenses when we are touched or when we sense our opponent is attacking. We have learned to react to the pressure of an outside force by automatically resisting it. In tai chi we work to change this reaction and to replace it by nonresistance, by yielding and neutralizing the incoming force. This neutralization process can cause the opponent, who expects but does not encounter resistance, to overextend and to lose balance. This giving up of our ingrained resisting response to a push or what appears to be our natural reaction to an attack for something else, even if the new pattern can be shown to be more serviceable, is very difficult and the work of some years.

If we see the value of and can achieve this physical letting go in push-hands, we might see that the same possibility for us exists in a mental or psychological release of beliefs we may have outgrown. There is really no separation between aspects of our being, like our body, mind, and spirit. Thus, because push-hands is not just a physical endeavor but incorporates all of what we are, what may look like only external practice can help us toward letting go on a number of deeper levels.

Finally, our hidden and unexamined ideas and beliefs about life may well retard or block our development, keeping us from breaking through the mental encrustations or the products of acculturation that prevent a clearer sight of reality. To help us get at truth or the reality that underlies the surface world with which most of us are concerned, we should be suspicious of the validity of the ideas our society favors about what life and the living of it is about. Especially is this desirable when we take into account Benjamin Lee Whorf's (see Chapter I) conclusion that the language we speak channels our thought processes in such a way that we see the world differently from people who speak a different language. We may need to depend less on language for our development in this crucial area and instead work in some other way to fashion our mind into an instrument that is open, flexible, and capable of concentration, if we hope to grasp the understandings the mystics and wise men over the millennia have said are there.

VI.

Development Made Possible By Push-hands

TAI CHI CHUAN IS a fighting system and is translated as Supreme Ultimate Fist. Push-hands training, if fighting skill is the object, can prepare you for fighting by teaching you to avoid or neutralize an opponent's attack and simultaneously counterattack. This is a highly refined method of fighting and takes years to develop. Instructions to students generally go as follows: An attack may take the form of a punch, kick, or strike, as well as an attempt to grab your clothing or some part of your body. Thus, if your face is the target of a punch, move your head to one side or the other, to the rear or possibly even duck under the punch in order to render it harmless. Simultaneously, counter with some response of your own, like a stiffened finger stab to the eyes or throat, a punch to the weakened, empty or *yin* side of the opponent's body, or a kick to some other exposed vulnerable area. Even if the opponent's punch should connect with your face, attempt to give with it enough to sustain only minimal damage while at the same time delivering a much more effective counterattack.

If an attack were limited to only one punch, you would, with continuous practice over time, be able to neutralize it and in the same instant counter effectively. Unfortunately, when we move to a more advanced level of sparring, where a punch may be just a feint designed to draw our defensive capability out of position and open us to a real attack, the situation becomes more complicated. Attacks may take the form of three or more punches and kicks delivered in rapid succession. In addition, the attacker may grasp some part of your body or your clothing, attempting to control your body position and your movement as he punches or kicks. He may sweep your foot to break your balance. If he has wrestling or judo training, he may attempt a takedown by ducking under your hands, grasping your knees or ankles, pivoting behind you, taking you down, and applying a submission hold or choke when you are on the ground.

The neutralization and simultaneous counterattack approach would prevail in any of the preceding situations if your level of skill were substantially above that of your opponent. For that matter, a far less accomplished opponent than you would probably be unable to successfully attack or defend against your attack even if you were not training yourself in a fighting method considered superior to most others. Along these lines, we know that, in general, a trained fighter can beat an untrained one. Also, other factors being fairly equal, a fighter trained in a more advanced fighting system will usually beat one whose training has been of lesser quality. But predictions about the outcome become more difficult when our mix includes such ingredients as strength, determination, and length and rigor of practice. Even an untrained fighter could have a good chance of beating a trained one if the former is much stronger, better coordinated, and in better shape than the latter. Though higher quality training will make a difference in a fight, it will not prevent defeat if your opponent is much stronger than you and is experienced in some rough fighting method. As for speed, although the speed with which an opponent delivers his attack is not in itself of great importance if it can be matched by your ability to respond, an attack moving at great speed leaves you with very little margin for delay or error.

To move to still another level, suppose your opponent has some skill in the use of an edged weapon. It may seem unfair to compare armed and unarmed combat, but a knife is easily concealed, can be brought into play rather quickly, and is considered an integral part of fighting equipment by those who train to fight in this way. Using a knife to fight is not so much different from hardening the hands in karate or training yourself to deliver a much stronger punch or kick than could an untrained person. No matter what you think about the fairness of fighting unarmed against someone with a knife, if you find yourself in this dangerous situation you will just have to react. But remember that neutralizing an attack involving just an opponent's hands and feet will, with the addition of a knife, almost certainly result in cuts or stab wounds. Conditions might be even worse for you if your attacker has a firearm and knows how to use it. Other than employing some form of magic, or the possibilities for evading bullets portrayed in movies, you will have no chance at all of neutralizing a well-aimed bullet or of getting within countering range before you are shot.

To return to the simple one-punch level, even here you need years of training to develop the reflexive response necessary to simultaneously neutralize and counterattack. When an attack occurs you have insufficient time to think of what is happening, to select an appropriate counter, and to execute your moves. A successful response must be instantaneous and must bypass conscious thought.

I have attempted in the foregoing few paragraphs to make the point that if becoming a good fighter is your primary goal, it is difficult and perhaps impossible to adequately prepare yourself through the practice of push-hands alone. The principles of push-hands are of great value in laying the foundations of a fighting system, but they must be supplemented by an equal amount of practice not only against pushes but against more sophisticated multiple attacks, including grappling, punches, strikes, and kicks. All of this practice is warranted if our goal is to develop fighting skill. If, however, fighting is not our primary objective, then we might spend our time more profitably practicing in a way that will enhance our development in other ways. Another reason for deemphasizing self-defense revolves around a point of view I put forward in *A Path to Liberation*. In effect, it is that our sense of personal security does not really depend on any skill we might have in defending ourselves from physical attack, but on the presence or absence of some inner development. If we do not, then, regard doing push-hands as preparation for fighting, what is its real value?

To put it simply, tai chi push-hands is the best training method I have found for helping students to see themselves and others more clearly, and to learn to live more completely in each moment without diluting these moments with thoughts of past or future. Coupled with the individual tai chi form, these training methods seem to help students' minds and spirits to open to a broader and deeper grasp of what life is about, and bring about behavior changes that benefit, or at least inflict minimal damage on, our lives and living space. All of this can come about without the injuries that invariably accompany the more intense and rigorous fighting training methods.

But I have found that these developments will not occur or even be approached unless you are willing, over many years of tai chi practice, to follow tai chi principles, perhaps most importantly that of nonresistance. Practicing push-hands gives us a chance to put Taoist philosophical principles to work in a way that goes beyond merely dealing with them as abstractions or as intellectual concepts, to incorporating them into our being.

To take the principle of nonresistance as an example, you are asked to respond to an opponent's attack by moving your body, and not your feet, in such a way that you offer no resistance to a blow or a push. This ability takes years to develop and you will go through many changes as you try to do it. At first you must use your conscious mind to direct your body to shift in such a way that a push misses its target. If you are mounting a simultaneous counterattack, this action also must receive conscious direction. Another aspect of pushing is the need to sense and to follow the opponent's center while, at the same time, denying him yours. The timing of your responses, also, must be correct. You can see that to think of and to sense all of these aspects of movement in the short time consumed by a push is not possible. You may be able to think of one or two of them, but the others have to be put, in a way, on automatic. Generally, you will focus on the aspect that gives you the most trouble—usually that of offering the push some degree of resistance. Though in your early years of training you will usually try to use your conscious mind to help you correct the flaws in your technique, eventually you will become increasingly able to make the right moves reflexively, without thinking. You have to learn to move in this way, because to think through your response will take you far too long and you will be either too slow or remain frozen in position. As you continue to practice, your physical and mental system will gradually learn to deal with an attack and your counterattack in a reflexive, direct, simple, and appropriate way.

Most students experience a number of similar reactions in their practice of push-hands. These reactions do not necessarily follow one another sequentially, and will be felt with greater intensity by some students than by others. Not surprisingly, students' physical and mental makeup largely determine their reactions to push-hands. Individual reactions will range from enjoyment of the physical and mental exchange to reluctance to face a confrontation accompanied by aggression or hostility in their opponent or in themselves.

After they learn the basic form of push-hands and are shown a few rudimentary responses to pushes, beginners will spend the next few months learning only to defend. We follow this pattern of instruction because defending and learning to neutralize is more difficult to learn than is attacking and pushing, although on a more advanced level both attacker and defender adhere to essentially the same principles of not pushing into resistance and of neutralizing an incoming force. At any rate, in their early training beginners will be defending with their backs to the wall (both literally and figuratively). In addition, in their escape attempts they will be disadvantaged in the sense that all of their opponents will be more skillful than they. One result of this pattern of practice is that beginners get almost no positive feedback from their efforts to offer no resistance and still escape a push. This situation can be somewhat frustrating, depending on students' attitudes to encountering constant failure over a number of months in something they are trying hard to accomplish.

To attempt to lessen this frustration, teachers will underscore the fact that students' ability and willingness to follow tai chi principles is of primary importance, rather than is actually evading a push or counterattacking. But relatively few students will really believe this and most, preoccupied with surface appearance, will be satisfied only with a successful evasion and counter. Those who have backgrounds in other martial arts may resort to those skills in an effort to avoid being pushed. The strong and athletic will use the powers they have attained. These students may not consciously choose to employ their abilities, but their training will come to the surface as a reflex when their opponent tries to push them. Therefore, martial arts training or other developed abilities are really an additional disadvantage in push-hands, because their possessors have to give up established and serviceable patterns for something new, different and, at the outset, ineffective.

The average beginning push-hands students, though they are told that they are engaged in an out-of the-ordinary training regimen, usually do not enjoy the constant failure that at first crowns their best efforts. They may begin to think of themselves as lacking in some form of intelligence, because of their inability to successfully evade an attack. Those with fragile egos sometimes give up their training altogether. Some who continue may mount a verbal counterattack, perhaps criticizing the opponent's aggressiveness or overuse of strength, to try to even the score and restore their self-esteem. Others will become angry with themselves or with their attacker. A few will stop trying and just accept their unskilled status as permanent. Students will demonstrate still other possibilities, as well as various combinations of those mentioned. All of these reactions must give way to a letting go of expectations and a temporary suspension of thinking and of attempting to analyze what is happening to them in tai chi. Beginners must simply continue their practice in the not unfounded hope that they will eventually be able to approach the level of skill demonstrated by their teacher and his advanced students.

When we are actually engaged in pushing hands we may find ourselves thinking about unrelated subjects or about irrelevant aspects of push-hands like an opponent's rigidity, failure to yield, aggressiveness, or whatever other faults he may appear to display. We must avoid allowing such thoughts to engage our attention and continue to attempt to concentrate on employing tai chi principles in our pushing. By this I mean, our awareness should register changes in our resistance, timing, balance, in the location of our center and the opponent's and so on. But we cannot hold all these elements in our mind at the same time and we will switch from one element to another as necessary. As stated above, ultimately we will not think about what we are doing but will sense opportunity and take appropriate measures earlier and earlier. If we see a danger or a flaw as it begins, we will have to make only a minimal change to counteract or to take advantage of it. On the other hand, once an attack or counterattack has a chance to develop or has gained some momentum we will need to take extreme measures to counter it or will fail altogether. Again, for best results we cannot depend on our normal thinking processes to react to split-second changes. We speak, then, in martial arts of having minds like still water, ready to reflect any change in a situation and to make an appropriate response. Naturally, any thinking we may do engages our attention and creates a small gap in our concentration that an opponent can exploit.

As suggested above, in this kind of difficult training, students will progress or develop optimumly if they give up all their notions of what they expect from their training, their positive or negative assessment of their mental and physical ability, and any ideas at all concerned with tai chi. They will have to learn to let go of conceptualizations of any sort, especially of attempts to try to use familiar words or symbols to explain to themselves or to others what push-hands is about. Until students develop some ability in push-hands, they will not know what concepts about push-hands mean even if they think they do. Moreover, the changes that their training can bring about will be slowed or distorted if they try to grasp the process intellectually through the means of their culturally based language. So it becomes a question of releasing earlier ideas or ways of explaining things in favor of simply practicing in the prescribed manner, until students gain enough experience to understand what is going on. Even then they may find it difficult or be unable to explain what they have learned or can do.

Another facet of push-hands training concerns our attitude toward our opponents or pushing partners. We might regard them primarily as persons we want to defeat or who threaten us in some way. After all, our interests seem opposed in that we want to unbalance them and they us. We may become angry with them if we feel that they are using unfair measures to win or that they are unnecessarily rough. They may serve as a convenient target for our dissatisfaction with our efforts or with our progress. Yet the most appropriate way to think of our opponents is with a large measure of gratefulness for the fact that they are there to help us develop. Without an opponent we would be unable to practice. Moreover, we might recognize that many of our flaws will be reflected in our opponents. For example, if we are hard and are using strength, our opponents will tend to do the same. If we soften up, they usually will, too. To take this interaction with opponents a step further, we might at some point in our training receive an intuitive flash about the interconnectedness of things, and the fallacy of considering ourselves separated from what is around us. This sense of things applies, of course, to our opponents and might well change the way we interact with them.

Obviously, we are learning much more in our training than to become more skillful in push-hands. As I said above, it is to our advantage to let go of the ideas about push-hands with which we began our training, because they are invalid and holding on to them will retard our development. As we get into pushing, we gradually respond to a push by giving way instead of resisting, a response that earlier seemed to go against our "natural" inclinations. With increased skill we will notice, as already stated, that what seems natural is really learned, can be unlearned, and replaced by a response that is possibly more adaptive. At any rate, we should not compartmentalize our tai chi, restricting it to the practice hall, but rather apply what we learn to our daily lives. Thus, letting go of ideas we have about how things are might allow us to be open to new and perhaps more useful ways of seeing the world. It's true that we might just replace one flawed way of seeing or assessing things with another equally flawed. On the other hand, the possibility is greater that we might learn to see things with additional clarity, though our seeing will be far from perfect.

In this vein, becoming aware of and developing our ability to change our conditioned response to some stimulus (not resisting a push) can be instructive and give us the confidence to attempt this in our everyday life. As suggested in an earlier chapter, it is of great benefit to us to escape our acculturation and to be, in a sense, reborn. We know that ways of relating to the world vary from culture to culture. From any particular society's standpoint the "right" way of seeing the world and of relating to what is around us is the way generally accepted in that society. It is quite probable that many of these ways of thinking of the world are mistaken or useful only in that society. Those who have lived for a time in a country other than their own may well have experienced "culture shock," which Webster's Dictionary defines as "a sense of confusion and uncertainty sometimes with feelings of anxiety that may affect people exposed to an alien culture without adequate preparation." Therefore, seeing more clearly requires a breaking of the hold on our minds of our cultural conditioning.

We want then to bring our push-hands training into our daily lives. In addition to the possibilities already suggested, this focus can take the form of our noticing the rise and fall of our thoughts and where warranted an examination of their content and origin. Our interaction with other people might also with profit undergo examination. We should not allow ourselves any form of delusion but as honestly as we can notice and recognize our feelings and motivations. Nor should we turn away from or fail to accept thoughts we might be ashamed of or find un-acceptable. It really is in our best interests to accept what is, rather than to deny it in favor of some sanitized distortion. If we want to change something in our lives that is within our power to change, we certainly are free to do so. Tai chi training can prepare us to pay this sort of close attention to what is going on in our lives.

VII.

Taoism and Tai Chi Chuan

BECAUSE TAOIST PHILOSOPHY is an important foundation of tai chi chuan, it may be useful to have some idea of what the *Tao Te Ching* (*Classic of the Way and Power*), the basis of Taoism, has to say. Scholarship relating to the Tao Te Ching, also known simply as the *Lao Tzu*, leans toward the view that this book may have been written in the fifth century B.C., but probably somewhat later, and that it is the work of not one but of a number of authors over a few centuries. The *Chuang Tzu*, thought to be a product of one or more men who lived in the fourth and third centuries B.C., might be said to have extended Taoist thought from the *Lao Tzu*'s more worldly concerns to the mystical. In fact, the ideas in the *Chuang Tzu* are believed to have had a strong influence on the Ch'an or Zen school of Buddhism. We need not get too excited about the history of these works and should not expect precision or even accuracy in establishing origins, precedence, and connectedness of writings and ideas 2,500 years ago in a culture vastly different from ours. Whatever the actual historical facts as to authorship or date of appearance, we should be content with having been given these philosophical thoughts for our edification, amusement and, above all, guidance.

As we read this material we should keep in mind that one of the Chinese ways of writing about philosophy, and perhaps a favored one, is to avoid exactness. Many writings, the *Lao Tzu* is an example, are composed mainly of disconnected aphorisms.

Authors made no attempt to set down their meaning unambiguously or to present arguments in a systematically reasoned way. This point was made by Fung, Yu-lan, a Chinese professor of philosophy in his book, *A Short History of Chinese Philosophy* (New York, The Macmillan Co., 1948). An additional factor contributing to what we might term the poetic character of Chinese writing is that it is comprised of ideographs that usually express a connotative as well as a denotative meaning. Thus, a thought presented in this way might be quite suggestive and full of implications, and be open to a number of interpretations. As for translations from Chinese to English, and to further underscore the point, a Chinese character can have the meaning of a number of English words.

Illustrating the potential of presenting a way of life in a suggestive rather than an unambiguous manner, the *Lao Tzu* is relatively short (a bit over 5,000 characters) but has formed the basis of a complete philosophical system. Commentators over the years have added their thinking to the basic treatise, gradually forming around it a whole body of additional supportive work. For us, who are unable to read these works in the original and who lack the background of the richness of meaning of Chinese characters, the suggestive aspect of the writings in translation might well be of greatest value. What the books appear to say, especially if the point of view presented can stimulate us to generate ideas beneficial to our society and to the world, is just as valuable as what the original authors may have actually meant. Moreover, if it is true that these men made it a point to avoid exactness of meaning, then they may well have intended readers to interpret their work freely within the fairly flexible parameters of the direction of their ideas.

The *I Ching* (*Book of Changes*) seems also to be the product of more than one hand and was probably written from the sixth to the third century B.C. Some say it appeared even earlier. The *I Ching* is one of the basic Confucian Classics and has exerted a great deal of influence on Chinese philosophical thought over the centuries. I mention the *I Ching* because both it and the *Lao Tzu* have as a basic premise the idea of reversal or return. That is, they taught that any movement that travels to its end must reverse itself. Chapter 40 in the *Lao Tzu* has the line, "Reversion is the action of Tao," and it is the Tao, unnameable and mysterious, which underlies surface reality and is the origin of everything. The concept of reversal may well have come from an observation of nature and the behavior of the sun, moon, and seasons, where the pattern followed is for something to get its start, gradually attain full flowering, and then to decline and die. From this basic foundation sprang a great many Taoist ideas concerning the way people should conduct their lives if they wished to preserve themselves and avoid injury.

To begin with, the *Lao Tzu* urges restraint and avoidance of any sort of extreme. So it becomes important in any endeavor to take care not to overdo. Intemperateness in doing anything is considered extreme and will have unwanted repercussions. Illustrations abound of overdoing, like our overshooting the flag or cup in golf because we hit the ball too hard, overeating and suffering the consequences of indigestion, going beyond our intended destination because we are unable to stop our vehicle in time, and so on. We also have to be careful not to underdo or we will fall short of whatever effect we hope to produce. However, underdoing, or better yet, leaving things alone seems to be favored over overdoing, because things are often running as they should be when we encounter them and mistakenly believe they need fixing. Our interfering in an ongoing process, therefore, also often produces some detrimental effect.

Unfortunately, for those of us who are looking for a set of blueprints for conducting our lives, the *Lao Tzu,* in avoiding precision or exactness, fails to tell us how to determine when we are applying too much or too little effort in attempting to accomplish a goal. Where timing and the time factor enter the picture we will encounter even more difficulty in deciding on when to apply effort and on how much effort over time is enough. What if we're trying for a long-term (over decades) result in some area? Obviously, there is no substitute for experience, especially in shorter-term matters, and for good judgment if we wish to make the right moves at the right time. Knowing that dangers are connected with overdoing and going to extremes goes only a certain distance toward keeping us from making incorrect decisions and suffering a reversal in our fortunes.

Another idea springing from the basic avoidance of extremes is that of simplicity. We are told to live as simply as possible instead of making our lives complicated. A desire to possess ever more things, to enjoy or undergo constantly changing or new experiences, and to have our gaze fixed not on what we are doing but on what might be of interest on the horizon are all examples of a kind of overdoing and are not conducive to our welfare. Contentment with what we have and with what we are doing seems connected with the suggestion to live life simply. We read in *Lao Tzu*, Chapter 46, "There is no calamity greater than lavish desires. There is no greater guilt than discontentment. And there is no greater disaster than greed."

Modesty is another favored attribute of Taoist thought. It rises from the idea that if we think we have accomplished a great deal in some field, or in life generally, we may well display an arrogance that is a kind of extreme leading to a decline. We must learn to hold back, lest overreaching, even in our thoughts, will have an effect opposite from one we desire. Remember, the *Lao Tzu* maintains that going as far as one can in one direction can't help but bring about movement in its opposite direction.

Yet another important aspect of Taoist philosophy as it relates to tai chi chuan and to push-hands in particular is that the soft, the yielding, overcomes the hard and rigid. *Lao Tzu*, Chapter 43, says, "The softest things in the world overcome the hardest things in the world." And Chapter 76, "When man is born, he is tender and weak. At death, he is stiff and hard. All things, the grass as well as trees, are tender and supple while alive. When dead, they are withered and dried." We may argue with these aphorisms and say they fail to withstand the scrutiny of logic. But their suggestion that softness, pliability, and flexibility are to human beings of greater value than rigidity and hardness is unarguable. Moreover, softness, flexibility of mind and body, and giving way are of great importance in doing push-hands effectively.

Some readers may feel that Taoist thought may place too much emphasis on the concerns of this world. Preserving life and preventing injury are certainly worthy pursuits, but those of us who sense the possibility of achieving a clearer understanding of reality might hope for additional emphasis on or a greater consideration of otherworldly themes.

Of course, the *Lao Tzu* does give such themes a measure of attention, beginning with the admonition that what underlies surface appearance is unnameable, inexplicable, and mysterious. Chapter 1 states, "The Tao that can be told is not the eternal Tao; the name that can be named is not the eternal name. The Nameless is the origin of Heaven and Earth." In Chapter 2 we have, " . . . the sage manages affairs without action and spreads doctrines without words." These ideas anticipate Ch'an or Zen Buddhist thought, especially the transmission of understanding without the use of words. Therefore, the *Lao Tzu* certainly has a strong mystical aspect as well as its more recognized this-worldly emphasis.

Nevertheless, scholars generally feel that the *Chuang Tzu* moves Taoism to a further stage of development in which the perfected man sees things from the standpoint of the Tao. He moves beyond seeing distinctions and opposites in the world to an appreciation of the connectedness and oneness of everything in the universe. Thus, the evolution of Taoist philosophy over the centuries is considered to have encompassed the transcendental and the mystical. The passage of time also witnessed the influence and effect on one another of Taoist and Buddhist thought. Here, again, it is difficult and perhaps nonproductive to attempt to accurately assess the degree and kind of influence on one another of these philosophies.

It seems evident that both Taoism and Ch'an Buddhism shared the ideas that we cannot put into words what the underlying reality is all about. Spiritual cultivation for human beings in these systems entailed doing one's daily work as well as possible without overdoing or underdoing and without attachment to results. When we live in this way we learn to give up making distinctions between things. We become one with the Tao. In this state, everything is part of everything else, all objects are imbued with spirit and the experiencer and experienced are one. Enlightenment may come when we have prepared the ground by living our lives without deliberate effort or particular intention. We may experience enlightenment suddenly or slowly over time and it will change our perspective to the extent that everything appears different. For example, problems we may have had will still be there, but we may no longer regard them as unpleasant and unwelcome intrusions in our life but in some way that indicates a recognition of their naturalness and perhaps usefulness in furthering our development. After achieving this breakthrough we continue with the seemingly pedestrian activities of everyday life but with the difference that our changed understanding of reality gives whatever we do a different significance.

This simple formulation of Taoist thought does not do justice to its breadth and depth. But my intention in this area is not to explore the many nuances of this philosophical system. Rather it is to get a sense of the basics of Taoist thought to help us to intuitively grasp the flavor of tai chi chuan, thereby strengthening our training and ultimately benefiting our lives.

Yet, the world is far from what it was two thousand and more years ago, and our culture is not Chinese. Some may believe that Taoist thought may be suitable only for a much simpler and far less sophisticated society than we have today. But perennial ideas about reality and the best way to live can often furnish us with different and refreshing perspectives on our problems, especially in areas where we realize that our lives have become too complicated. We may be looking for ways to reduce our many desires and the stress that accompanies our attempt to fulfill them. Many of us see also that we have gone too far in our exploitation of our finite resources, our poisoning of our environment and, the issue at the heart of most of our problems, our population growth. The Taoist view of the world or something like it might well help us to some kind of salvation.

Unfortunately, if we gain an intellectual grasp of the concepts presented in these Taoist books and we find the concepts valid and appealing, we will have taken only the first few steps toward bringing them into our lives. Given our Western belief in the value of rational and abstract thinking, we may feel that the way to know more about Taoist concepts is through scholarship. Therefore, we might spend our life attempting to determine the authorship of writings, learning Chinese in order to read extant manuscripts in the original and trying to decipher what their authors really meant. Such activities are not to be disparaged, because scholars are probably most responsible for unearthing, preserving, and translating works that have enriched our culture and increased our knowledge. They have stored the scholarship of both ancient and foreign cultures over the span of centuries, information and often wisdom which if not for their efforts would have been lost. But if our intention is to use the suggestions in these writings to change our lives in a positive way, we have to move beyond conceptualization or intellectualization.

Both the tai chi form and push-hands can help us to internalize the concepts found in these Taoist writings. As we practice daily, in accordance with the principles our teachers suggest, the Taoist ideas that underlie our training and that we recognize as useful somehow become a part of us. With the passing of sufficient time, we seem to react to life's unfolding in a way that accords with the philosophical ideas we favor. This process is the work of some years and is, in fact, never ending.

Focusing, then, on how all of this philosophy affects pushing hands, as explained above, an overriding consideration is to give up resistance. One reason for nonresistance is to invite your opponent to overextend, to allow his movement to come to an extreme, resulting in his loss of balance or his withdrawal. Another reason has to do with attempting to be soft and yielding, avoiding the hardness that is another example of an extreme. Additionally, if you have a chance to counterattack, do so with restraint and avoid overextending or allowing yourself to travel in some direction too far or too strongly. Keep movements simple and direct, rather than elaborate and circuitous. Use correct timing. If you are too early or too late in your moves, the result will be failure. Be careful not to overdo in pushing, but to use too little strength will also prove ineffective.

As you continue to practice pushing, you will concretely and physically experience rather than merely intellectually apprehend Taoist thought. You will see clearly that resistance to a push will almost always result in loss of balance or in some other undesired development. Overextension in any direction will disturb your balance. Bad timing will make any move ineffective and contribute to defeat. Elaborate moves usually take longer to perform and provide the opponent with additional opportunities, because your hands, usually in such instances, move too far away from your body. The further your hands stray from your body, the weaker your arms become and the more vulnerable your body is, because your hands and arms no longer form a protective shield to an attack. All of these lessons, constantly reinforced, and taking place on a mental as well as a physical plane, gradually bring you to a real understanding of what the Taoist concepts mean, and in experiencing their value serve to make it ever more possible to internalize them.

As for increasing or furthering your understanding of reality, if you practice push-hands without attachment to results and without expectations of any sort you will gradually come to a state of functioning without the use of your discriminating intellect. Your mind will not and really cannot draw distinctions of any sort as you push, because your reactions in attack and defense will then slow or stop altogether. It is this state of mind, of being fully in the moment, which prepares the ground for flashes of enlightenment or of seeing the world more clearly.

VIII.

The Push-hands Form

TAI CHI PUSH-HANDS ALLOWS, within certain bounds, for a great degree of creativity in attack and defense. Quite naturally, we introduce the boundaries at the outset when we ask opponents to face one another in the 70–30 stance, to avoid moving their feet and to adhere to a few prescribed ways of using their hands. Training may begin with our learning to lightly stick to only one of the opponent's hands, following it with one of our hands as it advances and withdraws. This one-hand pushing usually serves as an introduction to two-hands pushing, although some teachers may, in an attempt to reduce any possibility of the use of strength, resistance, and ego involvement generated by the presence of an opponent, limit their students to only this activity.

Restricting students to only one-hand pushing will, however, deny them the opportunity to experience the effect on themselves of facing an opponent who is trying to push them off balance and whom they want to push. If push-hands is simply a give-and-take exercise lacking the objective of pushing one another off-balance, students have no chance to taste the flavor of this confrontation, of being pushed despite their best efforts to avoid it, and of generally failing, over a long period of time, to do anything in push-hands effectively. Doing the individual form can help to center and calm them, but to retain this centeredness in the face of an adversary with opposing interests is much more difficult.

Some readers may wonder why I advocate two-hands pushing, given the negative things I have said about competition. In reply, I would say two-hands pushing need not be competitive if it is not set up as a contest to determine a winner and if we can, therefore, avoid the often harsh and ruthless mental attitude that accompanies training for contests or for fighting. In the practice hall, if training is correctly conducted, we are afforded a chance to engage in pushing with an opponent without thought about or attachment to the final outcome. Thus, accompanying the many benefits of push-hands of a more esoteric nature, mentioned in earlier chapters, are those possibilities for beneficial change of a seemingly more ordinary sort. For example, we can learn to recognize and release whatever nonproductive or negative preconceptions or feelings we have about confronting someone with an opposing agenda or point of view. Instead of acting burdened with this excess mental baggage we can learn to simply react reflexively to whatever is happening as well as we can. This training is absent from one-hand pushing.

Another point in favor of two-hands pushing is that in our society, like it or not, we must function in a competitive environment. It is valuable to learn to handle the confrontations we encounter each day in a way that allows us to hold our own while maintaining our equanimity.

Still another favorable aspect of this kind of push-hands is that it gives us a chance to know ourselves and our opponents in a very clear and direct way. Because we are so attached to language, we sometimes fail to penetrate the cloud of words we ourselves as well as others often use to mask or distort our real selves or intentions. Push-hands can cut through or get around all of this to give us a more direct view of ourselves and of our opponents. For example, if we believe and tell others that we love everyone and are laid-back and easygoing, only to find ourselves becoming angry and frustrated when we are pushed, this should at least cause us to curtail such statements as we come closer to recognizing our true feelings. We are afforded many opportunities to know ourselves and our opponents better through watching and registering reactions and feelings over the months and years of training.

Moving then to the push-hands form, whether pushing with one hand or two, opponents face each other squarely and assume the foot position of the 70–30 stance. Notice that in this stance the front foot points straight ahead and the back foot is turned at a 30-degree angle toward the front. Both knees are bent and remain bent as your weight shifts from one foot to the other. Let us call the man (without the mustache) on the right "**A**" and his opponent "**B**." **A** positions his front (right) foot so that his toe is even with **B**'s heel and his heel even with **B**'s toe. (Where one person's foot length differs markedly from the opponent's, they adjust their feet as well as they can to conform to the heel/toe arrangement.) In addition **A**'s front foot lines up with **B**'s back foot and his back foot lines up with **B**'s front.

The form of one-hand pushing requires that **A** raise his right hand, palm in, about eight inches in front of his solar plexus. **B** raises his right hand as well so that the backs of their hands lightly touch. (FIGURE 1.) Notice that the hand on the side of

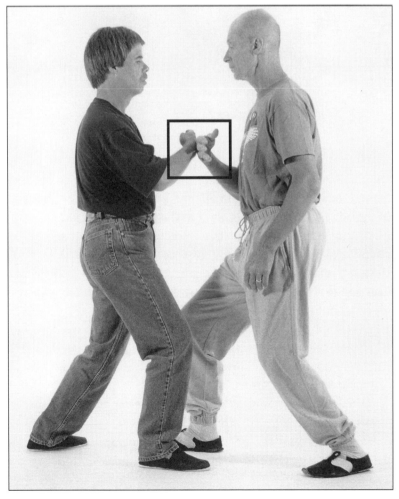

FIGURE 1

FIGURE 2

FIGURE 3

the advanced foot is used rather than the other. This is because the one-hand pushing form calls for a body rotation on the side of the advanced foot rather than to the less difficult side.

Because **A** is going to start the action, his weight should be mainly on his back foot and **B**'s weight mainly on his front. Ensure that throughout the exchange hands remain free of tension and that the movements come essentially from the legs and hips and not from the arms and shoulders.

As **A** shifts his weight onto his front foot and attacks **B**'s solar plexus with his right hand, **B** retreats and rotates his body to the right. (FIGURE 2.) **B**'s neutralization causes **A**'s hand to miss its target.

A becomes aware that he is losing the target and begins to withdraw his body and his hand. (FIGURE 3.)

In accord with the principle of adhering to the opponent's hand, **B** lightly sticks to **A**'s hand as it withdraws, moving his

FIGURE 4

FIGURE 5

weight toward his front foot, increasing his pressure on **A**'s hand and becoming the attacker, aiming for **A**'s solar plexus. **A** continues to shift his weight to the rear and rotates his body to the right to allow **B**'s attack to miss its target. (FIGURE 4.)

B withdraws and **A** once again resumes the attack. (FIGURE 5.)

During one-hand pushing keep the thumb on the pushing hand relaxed so that it drops close to the palm and does not stick up. Relax the arm and hand not in use and allow it to hang naturally at your side. When the opponent increases pressure, release your pressure, move your body, neutralizing his push, until his attack misses and he is forced to withdraw. Fill this vacuum by sticking to the withdrawing hand and attacking. Try throughout the attack and withdrawal to adhere lightly to the back of the opponent's hand. When it is your turn to attack and you slightly increase your hand pressure, should the oppo-

FIGURE 6

FIGURE 7

nent resist your push, you could slip past his rigid hand and go directly to his body. (FIGURE 6.)

Resistance should not enter the picture at all, however, because one-hand pushing usually has the function of allowing you to get a feel of hands sticking to each other through the advance and withdrawal of attack and defense. It can promote, also, body flexibility as you shift weight and rotate to avoid an attack.

Throughout the exercise keep your knees bent so that your height is the same as in the one-quarter squat you maintain in the tai chi form. Be especially aware of your back leg as your weight shifts forward and avoid allowing the knee of the back leg to straighten.

Attack and defense in one-hand pushing can continue indefinitely. A freer give-and-take than the suggested one can develop if targets for attack are not limited to the solar plexus. The attack could be directed at the opponent's head or to his lower

FIGURE 8   **FIGURE 9**

abdomen. (FIGURE 7.) Whatever the target, keep the action slow and respond by withdrawing and rotating your body, thereby neutralizing the attack.

Be sure in practice to give equal attention to both sides of your body and avoid favoring one side over the other. If you advance your left foot, use your left hand to push. Rotate your body to the left when neutralizing if your left foot is forward. (FIGURE 8.)

In two-hands pushing, opponents face each other as they did in one-hand pushing. **A**'s weight is 70 or more percent on his front foot as he places his left forearm, palm facing in, in front of his body at solar plexus level and about eight inches away. **B**'s weight is mostly on his back foot. **B** puts his left palm on **A**'s left wrist and cups **A**'s elbow with his right palm. At the same time, **A** places his right elbow near **B**'s left elbow. **A**'s right forearm is close to vertical and his fingers point up. (FIGURE 9.)

FIGURE 10

FIGURE 11

B begins to shift his weight from his back foot toward his front and initiates a push. **A** retreats toward his back foot and rotates his body to the left, neutralizing **B**'s push. Simultaneously, **A** lightly counters with elbow pressure against **B**'s left elbow. (FIGURE 10.)

Were **B** to continue pushing without changing direction he would overextend and lose his balance. (FIGURE 11.)

The push-hands form prescribes that before **B** loses his balance he becomes aware that he has lost **A**'s center. He responds by turning his left hand and placing its back against **A**'s left wrist, and moves his right hand to his left palm, shifting more of his weight to his front foot and attacking the new location of **A**'s center. (FIGURE 12.)

A replies to **B**'s change of direction by rotating his body to the right, shifting his weight further to his back foot, and lowering his right hand to the back of **B**'s right wrist. (FIGURE 13.)

FIGURE 12

FIGURE 13

If **B** continued his attack and **A** helped him in that direction by lightly pulling on his wrist and elbow, **B** would again lose his balance. (FIGURE 14.)

According to the push-hands form, **B** becomes aware in time of his possible overextension and begins to withdraw. **B** now assumes the role of defender as he places his right forearm eight inches in front of his solar plexus, palm in, ready to receive or relate to **A**'s attacking hands. As **B** withdraws, **A** rotates his right palm on **B**'s right wrist and cups **B**'s right elbow with his left palm. **B** raises his left hand and places his left elbow near **A**'s right elbow. These hand

FIGURE 14

FIGURE 15

FIGURE 16

movements accompany the beginning of a weight shift on the part of both opponents and the rotation of **B**'s body. (FIGURE 15.)

To neutralize **A**'s push, **B** continues to rotate his body to the right and to shift his weight toward his back foot. At the same time, **B** exerts light pressure with his left elbow against **A**'s right elbow. (FIGURE 16.)

Were **A** to continue his attack in the same direction he would lose **B**'s center, would overextend and lose his balance. (FIGURE 17.)

Sensing the necessity for a direction change, **A** rotates the hand on **B**'s wrist until the back of his hand touches **B**'s wrist and places his left palm on his right. **A**'s weight continues to shift toward his front foot as he attacks the new location of **B**'s center. (FIGURE 18.)

B replies to **A**'s new attack by continuing to withdraw to his back foot and rotating his body to the left. At the same time **B** lowers his left hand to **A**'s left wrist. (FIGURE 19.)

Were **A** to continue his attack, he would overextend and lose his balance. (FIGURE 20.)

A must withdraw and **B** becomes the attacker. (FIGURE 21.)

FIGURE 17

FIGURE 18

FIGURE 19

FIGURE 20

FIGURE 21

Throughout the two-hands form and generally as you break the form to push more freely, keep your hips square to the opponent when you attack and rotate them appropriately when you defend. Avoid doing the form in a mechanical way, as if it were merely a preliminary set of movements preceding serious pushing. Skillful students pushing with those less skilled can neutralize and counter attacks using only the movements demonstrated in the push-hands form description. In theory, also, two skillful and evenly matched opponents might continue the form through many exchanges as they fail to find an opening for a successful attack and are able to sense and correct a weakness in their own position before the opponent can exploit it. Nevertheless, in practice do only a couple of rounds of the push-hands form before you attempt a definitive attack. But do these initial rounds attentively, as if they matter.

If your attention strays you may fail to notice that as you retreat your body does not rotate as it should from one side to the other, but instead remains square to the opponent. One reason for failure to do the push-hands form correctly is that you may be exchanging social pleasantries in this initial portion of push-hands. Keep talk to a minimum, or avoid it altogether, because meditative concentration cannot but suffer when your mouth is moving and your thoughts are on subjects unrelated to push-hands, or for that matter, on anything at all. Save social interaction for times when you are not practicing.

Another common error in the push-hands form as you defend is failure to notice your transfer of weight from your front to your back foot. If you use up all your space and shift all of your weight to your back foot on the first half of the opponent's attack (push phase), you will be vulnerable at the moment you attempt to rotate your body in the opposite direction to neutralize the change in direction of the opponent's attack (press phase). To rotate and neutralize successfully you must retain some ability to shift your weight to the rear. As a general rule, accomplish half of your possible shift of weight from one foot to the other in the push phase of the form and the other half in the press phase.

IX.

Main Considerations in Push-hands

LET US NOW TURN TO THE actual mechanics of pushing hands and discuss those points that will help you to learn and to improve in push-hands. Because an unclear or unfamiliar term, or an explanation, used in an earlier point may be treated more elaborately in a later one, read all of these considerations before coming back to some that may at first reading seem obscure or difficult to understand. Also, since many of the suggestions will concern actions that are in play simultaneously, becoming familiar with the whole list will give an appreciation of their interrelatedness. To begin:

1. Avoid Moving Your Feet

My teacher, Cheng, Man-ching, emphasized the importance of
not moving your feet if you wish to learn to neutralize attacks by
appropriate shifts of your body. Were you permitted to step away
to avoid a push you would lose the opportunity to work on
developing a timely adjustment of your body to render the attack
harmless. Having the option of moving your feet is of value if
you are training for fighting, but a fixed-foot way of practicing
push-hands is perfectly suitable to enable you to attain the
benefits described in earlier chapters. You can do push-hands
into old age as long as you can stand and shift your weight from
foot to foot.

There are minor exceptions to the fixed-foot rule. In defending, if your weight moves to your back foot and your
body rotates so that you present your side to the attacker, it is
permissible to turn out the toe of the back foot until the knee is
comfortably over the foot. (FIGURE 22.) Turn the toe again to a
30-degree angle toward the opponent, if your counterattack
causes your opponent to retreat. In addition, when attacking an
opponent who may have taken a longer than usual stance and
has retreated to his back foot (FIGURE 23), you are allowed to
slide your front foot forward about six inches simultaneously
with the completion of your push. (FIGURE 24.) Sometimes in
their escape attempt defenders turn out their back foot's toe and
then, instead of turning the toe back in as they should, move the
heel further back. They will often follow this with another toe
turnout. This back-foot movement lengthens their stance. Your
forward slide provides a bit of additional extension to counteract such an opponent's extreme withdrawal. Slide forward also
when using your forearm to push, because a forearm push
reduces your reach to the length of your upper arm instead of all
the way to your hand. (FIGURE 25.)

Another reason for sliding your front foot forward if you
need additional extension is that your front knee should not go
more than an inch or so beyond your toes. Tai chi *Classics* state
that allowing the front knee to move beyond the toes weakens
your stance. However, the knee's inch or so extension beyond
the toes seems in my experience not to detract from the attack's
effectiveness.

FIGURE 22

FIGURE 23

FIGURE 24

FIGURE 25

2. Study and Use These Offensive and Defensive Tactics

Let us begin with opponents facing each other in the 70–30 stance, their right foot advanced. When an opponent departs from the push-hands form and begins a more concerted attack, you will have begun rotating your body and begun withdrawing to your back foot. Therefore, he will usually place one of his hands on the middle of your chest and the other on your side, or on your upper arm, which shields your side, halfway between your shoulder and elbow. (FIGURE 26.) Many fighting systems advocate using your hands and arms to fend off these attacking hands, but this method is not the tai chi one. Rather, as in the push-hands form, continue to use your hands and arms to stick to the opponent's hands and move whatever part of your body is targeted so that if the attack developed fully, it would miss or be neutralized.

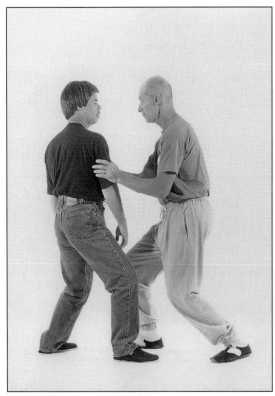

FIGURE 26

FIGURE 27

The reason for your body rotation at the instant you sense an attack is that one of your opponent's hands will probably come to your chest and may suddenly and explosively push there, with the potential of causing injury. Your rotation will remove your chest from a direct attack and present your side to the opponent, but here your arm is usually between your body and the attacking hand, making injury less likely.

As you defend, keep your body in this half-front facing position, with your side facing your opponent. If you sense a strong push from the hand on your chest avoid rotating your body to the opposite side as you attempt to neutralize. (FIGURE 27.) Instead, neutralize by a slight lateral body movement to avoid the attack, at the same time withdrawing further and perhaps bending at the waist and bending your knees additionally. (FIGURE 28.) Although you may neutralize success-fully by rotating to the opposite side, you become vulnerable to the opponent's elbow strike at the moment in the rotation when you face him squarely. (FIGURE 29.)

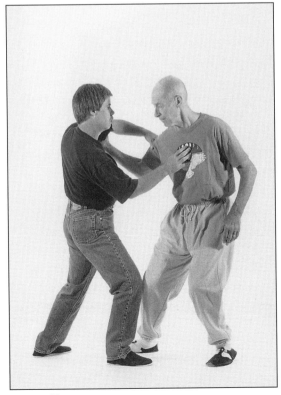

FIGURE 28   **FIGURE 29**

FIGURE 30

FIGURE 31

Keeping the above points in mind, let's continue with the defense. As you turn your waist to present your right side to your opponent, bring your right hand to your opponent's left side or his left elbow if it is covering his side. (FIGURE 30.) The opponent will have started his attack with his weight mostly on his back or left foot and will be advancing, moving his weight onto his front or right foot. The instant his weight becomes equal between his left and right foot, an unavoidable position when his weight shifts from one foot to the other, he will be "double-weighted" and vulnerable to a lateral push (your right hand on his left elbow). Simultaneously with your neutralization of your opponent's attack, push with your right hand very lightly toward his right rear quadrant. Find and remain on the opponent's center as you counterattack. As your experience and skill increase you will learn to neutralize the opponent's push by a slight body adjustment and simultaneously to apply the lateral counter. (FIGURE 31.)

Your opponent now has a number of options, but let us address the one most commonly followed. In this instance, as you attempt your lateral counter, your opponent will neutralize it by a slight body rotation or a body bend, thereby emptying

FIGURE 32

FIGURE 33

his left arm or side, and continue his attack with his right hand, which is positioned on your chest. (FIGURE 32.) Neutralize this push by further rotating your waist, withdrawing to your left foot, bending at the waist, and bending your knees still further. You can do these body movements individually or combine them as you see fit. As you neutralize, lightly catch the opponent's right wrist with your left hand and bring your right hand from his left elbow to just above his right elbow. Your right wrist contacts the opponent's upper arm with your palm facing in. You now have secured an arm bar on the opponent's right arm that you can use to unbalance him by maintaining most of your weight on your back foot and rotating your hips to the right, pulling lightly on his upper arm as you rotate. (FIGURES 33, 34,

FIGURE 34

FIGURE 35

FIGURE 36

FIGURE 37

FIGURE 38

35, and 36 illustrate these actions.) However, avoid forcing the action. Try to sense the direction the opponent wants to go and, with the arm bar, help him to go that way until he loses his balance. For example, if he withdraws follow him and push with your right forearm. (FIGURE 37.) The opponent may attempt to continue his forward movement to push you with his shoulder despite your having caught his right arm. In this instance rotate your body to the right to neutralize his push and with minimum strength raise his right wrist as you pull forward on his upper arm. He will lose his balance to the front. (FIGURE 38.) If you notice that the opponent is recovering his balance, or that the arm bar has become ineffective, do not hesitate to release his arm and to switch your right hand back to his left elbow, trying again for a lateral push. (FIGURE 39.) You may find yourself switching back and forth a few times between the opponent's right arm and left side before you successfully complete your counterattack. To facilitate switching, avoid flexing or tightening your arm in your effort to secure an arm bar or to off-balance the opponent. Instead, keep your arm relaxed and loose.

Another possible reply on the opponent's part to your lateral counter, especially if he senses that you are on his center and close to successfully breaking his balance, is to shift his weight further forward, rotating his body to the left to neutralize your push on his elbow. At the same time he will catch your upper right arm with his right wrist and your right wrist with his left hand. (FIGURE 40.)

FIGURE 39   **FIGURE 40**

FIGURE 41

FIGURE 42

He will then immediately rotate his body to the right, shifting almost all of his weight to his back foot and pulling lightly with his right wrist against your right upper arm. The result of his move will be to off-balance you to your front. (FIGURE 41.) However, his counter will be successful only if you lose his center in your attempt to counter him laterally. If you stay on his center and follow him through the beginning of his attempted counterattack, you can unbalance him as he shifts to his front foot. (FIGURE 42.)

Still another possible exchange can occur when your opponent misses your center as he pushes on your arm with his left hand. We will assume that his push missed its intended target because you shifted your body in a timely way and that he pushed too hard. (FIGURE 43.) As soon as he became aware of his coming off the center he should have continued his attack on the new location of your center, sliding his front foot slightly forward and using his left forearm and elbow to attack your side. (FIGURE 44.) However, if he put too much into his push on your upper arm you can catch his left wrist with your left hand and lightly pull his left arm in the direction it is pushing. (FIGURE 45.) If the opponent notices his predicament and begins to withdraw, follow him, retaining a light hold on his wrist, and with your right hand push his left side to his diagonal right rear. (FIGURE 46.)

FIGURE 43

FIGURE 44

FIGURE 45

FIGURE 46

FIGURE 47

Counterattacks have the best chance of success if they are launched while the opponent's mind, or his intent, is on his attack. If you can neutralize the attack, the opponent may be too concerned with getting back on your center to notice that you have begun a countermove.

If your counterattack is not immediately or fully successful but is effective enough to cause your opponent to break off his attack and to retreat, immediately change your body position from the defending one in which you presented your side to your opponent to one in which you face him squarely. At the same time, shift your center of gravity forward to fill the vacuum created by your opponent's retreat and place one hand on his chest and the other on his upper arm. (FIGURE 47.) Pursue your attack to completion. To sum up this particular exchange the *Classics* say, "You yield at your opponent's slightest pressure and adhere to him at his slightest retreat."

The foregoing are typical push-hands exchanges that will occur over and over. However, no two attacking or defending moves are ever exactly the same, though they may appear so to the casual eye. There seem to be an infinite number of slight variations on each basic move. Beginners may practice the suggested defensive tactics thousands of times without success, because their more skillful opponents are better able than they to sense their movements and will make appropriate adjustments in their attack. But beginners must maintain faith that each time they attempt these maneuvers, especially in the way tai chi principles prescribe, their development is proceeding.

3. Maintain Flexibility in Your Body Position

Generally speaking, the number of options for movement in any direction are greatest when your body is perpendicular to the ground. From this position you can most easily rotate your body from side to side, bend forward and backward, and to either side. But you need not remain in this perpendicular position when you are pushed, because you might be able to neutralize your opponent's attack at the right moment by a bending away or hollowing out of the targeted area. Thus, a jackknifing at the waist accompanied by a further bending of the knees might well cause your opponent to overextend and allow you to counterattack. Break your perpendicular stance for just a moment and then return to it. The object is to neutralize the attack and simultaneously to counterattack. (FIGURE 48.)

FIGURE 48

FIGURE 49

FIGURE 50

An additional bending of your knees may well accompany each of your countermoves. Your knees are already bent in about a one-quarter squat as a part of your normal stance in the push-hands position, but a sudden additional knee bend serves to help you withdraw further from, or move your center of gravity under, the opponent. The effect of this surprise drop, even though it may be only a matter of a couple of inches, is to give you a bit more leeway in your counterattack, because the opponent will tend to keep his hands on you and allow his arms to straighten additionally. Position before dropping. (FIGURE 49.) Position after dropping and after securing the arm bar afforded by your opponent's straightening arm. (FIGURE 50.) Straightening the elbows tends to weaken the arms and make them more vulnerable to attack. The opponent's best response to your sudden drop would be to drop his body with yours, thus keeping your heights and the position of his hands and arms relatively the same. But no matter how alert he is to your body drop, he will delay a split second in his response and you could use this time and the change in the position of his arms to your advantage.

Immediately after dropping, whether or not your counter-attack succeeded, return to your earlier level. If the initial portion of your counter was successful, you can complete it at this level. If your countermove failed, you are back to your initial level and have a chance to drop once more as you try another counterattack.

Avoid bending your knees to such an extent that you are unable to easily rise to your earlier level. Especially avoid a full squat in your effort to neutralize an attack. (FIGURE 51.) Your opponent in this situation can roll you backward. (FIGURE 52.) If he needs added extension he can slide his front foot forward as he completes his attack. Remember, too, that the lower you squat the less flexibility of response you will retain.

FIGURE 51

FIGURE 52

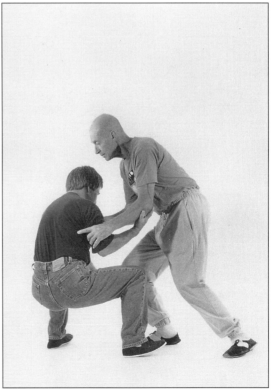

4. Avoid Using Strength

We are told in push-hands that we should be able to deflect the momentum of a thousand pounds with a trigger force of four ounces. Of course, some physical strength must go into a push or a countermove if you are to unbalance the opponent. The question is, how much strength should you use? The more strength you exert the greater chance you have of losing your own balance should your opponent be able to neutralize your move. This danger alone should be enough to restrain your enthusiasm. You may argue that using minimal strength will result in a weak push. But this need not be true if you have correctly maneuvered your opponent into a position where he has momentarily lost his balance or is on the edge or at the outer limit of his position. If you are able to sense such a weakness in the opponent's stance, it will take only a very light push to break his balance.

In pushing, as stated above, one of your hands should be placed in the middle of your opponent's chest (your hand should

FIGURE 53

FIGURE 54

FIGURE 55

be slightly higher if your opponent is a woman) and the other on his upper arm halfway between elbow and shoulder. Avoid putting a hand on the shoulder instead of on the arm, because the opponent's shoulder can be like a ball and, in this rounded form, quite slippery. (FIGURE 53.) Also, do not put both hands on your opponent's arm, one above the other. (FIGURE 54.) If the opponent turns his waist, both hands will lose the center and the hand normally positioned on the opponent's chest will be unable to return there in time to push the new location of the body's center. (FIGURE 55.)

You will encounter the same problem if, in your attack, you remove one of your hands from the opponent. Usually, this occurs when (FIGURE 56.) you are

FIGURE 56

FIGURE 57

FIGURE 58

pushing your opponent's side or arm, if it is covering his side, with your left hand and you take away the hand on the opponent's chest, thinking it is of little importance. If your opponent rotates his body to neutralize your left-hand push, the split second you will need to place your right hand on his chest and to regain the center with that hand may be enough to allow your opponent to take control. (FIGURES 57 and 58.)

Push with only one hand at a time. Rest the hand not pushing lightly on the opponent's chest or arm and be ready to bring it into play if the situation should suddenly change. If you push the opponent's arm and he resists, instantaneously switch your effort to the hand on the chest, emptying, or not pushing with, the hand on the arm but not removing it. The push will then come from a different angle and will either break the opponent's balance partially or completely. If his reaction is quick enough and he begins to resist the chest push, instantaneously switch back to the arm, leaving the hand in position on the chest but exerting no pressure. In the meantime your body will have con-

FIGURE 59

FIGURE 60

tinued to move forward and the opponent's body to the rear as he is forced to give ground or suffer the loss of balance. After one or more of these changes in the direction of your attack, your opponent will have retreated to the point where his position will have become weak. Just a small push will then be enough to send him off balance.

At no point in your attack need you use an appreciable amount of strength. Encountering resistance is no reason to increase your pressure. Instead, attack lightly from a different angle. Another option when attacking and encountering resistance is to withdraw slightly and then instantly, using the same hand, to resume the push. This slight withdrawal causes the opponent to tip a bit forward as the push he is resisting suddenly disappears. He is vulnerable to a push as he momentarily hangs there. The opponent is slightly off balance when the push on his arm he resisted is suddenly withdrawn. (FIGURE 59.) He is subject to push as attack resumes. (FIGURE 60.)

When defending and attempting a lateral counterattack at

FIGURE 61

FIGURE 62

the instant the attacker becomes double-weighted, avoid keeping your hip forward on the side of the arm used to counter. (FIGURE 61.) Withdraw your hips and retain the capability of shifting them from side to side to neutralize the opponent's push and to keep him off your center. (FIGURE 62.) Students keep their leading hip forward in the mistaken idea that it will strengthen their position and facilitate their lateral counterattack. But only minimal strength is necessary to off balance the attacker if your timing and direction are correct. Work on developing these aspects of your counter and withdraw your hips, allowing them the movement necessary to neutralize the attack.

5. Remain Relaxed

"Remain relaxed" means that you use only those parts of your body necessary to an action, removing strength or tension from the muscles not in play. Your tai chi form practice will help you develop your ability to release unnecessary tension. If you are unable to relax when attacking, you will have great difficulty in changing your push quickly from one hand to the other. When defending you will probably present the attacker a rigid or hard surface that he can use to advantage as his attack develops. If you are tense you will waste your energy and tire more quickly. Your moves will usually be stiffish and you will be slower to respond, because in order to move you will first have to unfreeze from your rigid position. This unfreezing takes a split second, but this lost time usually makes for a delayed response.

As stated earlier, the tai chi chuan *Classics* tell us we must let our *chi* (intrinsic energy) sink to the *tan t'ien* (lower abdominal area). Relaxing plays an important part in making this sinking possible. If we are tense, often our chi will be in our arms and shoulders and our body's center of gravity will be too high, making us top-heavy and our balance more easily disturbed. In addition, our attack will lack the kind of wavelike power that flows from the feet into the legs and is directed by the hips through the upper body to the hand and onto the target.

6. Use Correct Timing

This consideration seems fairly obvious. If your timing is faulty, if you move too early or too late, your attack or defense will fail. As suggested above, remaining relaxed will better enable you to respond in a timely way to your opponent's movements. Tension in your body will inhibit a quick reply to a perceived opening. Your countermoves will have a much greater chance of success if you make them at the same time you neutralize the opponent's attack. Avoid a 1–2 kind of response in which you first neutralize and then attempt your counter. In this scenario your opponent may realize his error as you neutralize and make a correction, continuing his attack before you can counterattack.

The question of speed in relation to timing is an interesting one. Students often say that their teacher moves so much more quickly than they, that they are never in time. But it is not that the teacher moves faster than they and that to hold their own they will have to do whatever they do more quickly. Instead, the teacher moves earlier than the student, because he is able to sense a weakness or an opening before the student becomes aware of it. What appears to the student as speed of execution really has to do with getting an earlier start. As students become more sensitive, the action will seem to slow down and they will sense opportunities much sooner than they did in their first years of practice.

Some have said that we should attempt to anticipate our opponent's moves and that we will then be able to make necessary adjustments in our position to nullify the opponent's attack when it comes. "Anticipate" here is misunderstood if it means that we consciously notice that our opponent plans to make some move and that we choose and begin a countermove in an attempt to forestall him. This conscious noticing and initiating a response is not the way push-hands works. Rather, without thinking, we may sense a subtle change in our opponent's position and in response to the sensing make some sort of instantaneous reply. We may appear to have anticipated our opponent's move, but in reality have merely responded appropriately, as usual, to whatever the unfolding situation required.

FIGURE 63

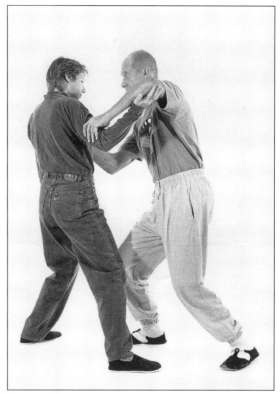

FIGURE 64

An example of mistakenly employing anticipation occurs when your opponent is defending against an attack. Let us assume that he will move toward his back foot, rotate his body, and attempt a lateral counterattack at the instant you become double-weighted. (FIGURE 63.) Your response to his counter would probably be to neutralize his lateral counter and simultaneously attack with the hand on his chest. (FIGURE 64.) He may "anticipate" this push against his chest and lean into your push while trying to continue his lateral counterattack. (FIGURE 65.) Here he would not only be violating the tai chi principle of nonresistance but go even a step further by beginning to

FIGURE 65

FIGURE 66

resist a push that has not yet started. As soon as you notice his lean, use the hand on his arm to help him gently in the direction of his lean and he will lose his balance. (FIGURE 66.)

As for your general speed of movement in push-hands, attempt to slow the action so that you and your opponent are better able to notice what you are doing. Moving slowly will enable you to become aware of your resistance to a push, of your inability to evade or neutralize, and of many other aspects of attack and defense. However, you must adjust your speed to that of your opponent. If he moves slowly so must you, and if he moves quickly you must follow suit or be overwhelmed. Attempting to keep the action slow when your opponent speeds up will obviously delay all of your responses to an attack or a defensive counter.

Increasing your speed when your opponent is moving slowly can have a number of causes. Perhaps you sense an opening of some sort and don't want to miss the chance to exploit it. You may notice a mistake you are making and wish to correct it before your opponent can take advantage of it. You may believe that by moving slowly you will give your opponent more time to counter your attack. But all of these reasons are poor excuses for speeding up when weighed against the possible loss of control and the greater possibility of overdoing that accompanies increased speed.

7. *Learn to Sense the Location of the Body's Center*

When we speak of the "center" in tai chi we refer to that point on the body where a push will be exactly on target. Imagine that you are pushing a ball across the floor. The ball will rotate in various directions and you will have to adjust your push to remain on its center and to keep it moving in the direction you want it to go. In pushing with an opponent, if you are attacking try to stay on his center from the beginning to the conclusion of your push. If you lose his center you will be momentarily disoriented until you find it again. This gap or lapse affords the opponent a chance for a counterattack. The amount of strength you use in pushing and your speed are both secondary to your ability to remain on your opponent's center. Your attack will be ineffective, whether pushing or punching, if you miss your target or fail to contact it solidly. As you attack be careful that the instant you become double-weighted the opponent does not find your center and begin a counterattack. If you are defending, you must sense the direction of the attack and move your center in such a way that the push will miss, while simultaneously trying to get on the opponent's center and take control.

FIGURE 67

All of these actions may take place in less than a second, although (see #6) in our training we try to slow the action down. By moving more slowly we are better able to "listen" and to feel what is happening. We will gradually gain an awareness of how an attack develops, whether it is on our center and what moves we are making to evade, neutralize, and counter. Developing this ability is, without exaggeration, the work of years. Therefore, beginners should not be discouraged if they seem to have little success in their first year or two of practice. Push missing the center. (FIGURE 67.) Push on center. (FIGURE 68.)

FIGURE 68

8. Avoid Straightening Your Elbows

Keep your elbows bent and slightly in advance of your body as you attack. Use your hands as sensors as you attempt to find and stay on your opponent's center. Try to detect the changes in all of your opponent's responses to your attack, ranging from resistance to attempted counterattacks, and deal appropriately with them. Little by little you will be able to detect and reply to these changes instantaneously or reflexively rather than with conscious thought. As your opponent shifts away to evade you or loses balance, avoid pushing too far with either hand so that even though your opponent moves away, your elbows remain bent. In other words, if your opponent withdraws close the distance between you by moving your body forward (FIGURE 69),

FIGURE 69

FIGURE 70

rather than by straightening your elbows and leaving your body behind. (FIGURE 70.) There should be less occasion for your elbows to straighten if you keep the distance between you and your opponent constant. Finally, complete your push by triggering or releasing a small amount of energy at precisely the right time and on the right spot. The opponent then will be propelled away from you, making an elbow-straightening follow-through unnecessary. Correct completion of push, elbows remain bent. (FIGURE 71.) Incorrect follow-through of push, elbows straightened. (FIGURE 72.)

If your idea of pushing is not a triggered small burst of energy on the target with correct timing, but rather a continuous effort for a seemingly more effective push, it is likely that in the process you will straighten your elbows. Although your opponent will have been pushed, if we examine the larger picture you will have allowed your hands to stray too far from your body to

FIGURE 71   **FIGURE 72**

FIGURE 73

FIGURE 74

block kicks or punches to body targets. Thus, you will have made yourself vulnerable to the opponent's kick if he were able to step back early enough to compensate for the loss of balance caused by his inability to neutralize your push. (FIGURE 73.)

The arms often straighten when you push by keeping your hips back and leaning forward instead of by remaining fairly perpendicular and pushing, in effect, from the *tan t'ien*. It may seem that you are playing it safe by keeping your hips away from the opponent and pushing by extending your arms. (FIGURE 74.) Unfortunately, this method of pushing raises your center from the tan t'ien region toward your shoulders, adversely affecting your balance, and as explained in the preceding paragraph, affords your opponent, even if you push him, an opening for a possibly incapacitating kick.

9. *Attack Correctly and Effectively*

The general method of correct attack is as follows: shift your weight steadily toward the opponent, establishing and maintaining your push on the center. The opponent will usually retreat until he runs out of space and has his weight almost completely on his back leg. At that instant he may well resist your push because he has nowhere to go. As described above, allow him a split-second's reprieve by withdrawing a fraction of an inch and then complete your push. This method gives far better results than pushing through the opponent's resistance. In addition, at the instant you withdraw a bit the opponent slightly loses his balance when the push he is trying to resist disappears. At that moment he is most vulnerable to a finishing push. You can also finish the push by changing the hand doing the pushing. (see #4.) For example, if you are pushing with your left hand and encounter resistance, instantaneously switching to the right hand while emptying the left may well break your opponent's balance. Keep both hands on your opponent (usually one on his chest and one on his upper arm) as you perform this switch in applying energy.

Even when you are on the opponent's center, you can get a better result in your final push by attacking slightly downward or diagonally downward instead of horizontally. A slight additional bending of your knees toward the conclusion of your push will facilitate this downward push. It will also further lower your center of gravity, increasing your stability, and making it more difficult for the opponent to suddenly drop lower and counterattack. This downward push serves to break the opponent's "root" and sends him up into the air. Although this effect may seem more spectacular or indicate greater efficaciousness in your push, what is most important from the standpoint of fighting is the opponent's loss of balance. In sparring where foot movement is permitted, opponents learn to sense an impending loss of balance soon enough to change, by moving one or both feet, to a stronger and better balanced stance from which they can block and counter an attack. In tai chi where we are not allowed foot movement, we avoid losing balance by moving the part of our body targeted for attack, hoping our opponent will overextend and overbalance in his unsuccessful attack and provide us a chance to counterattack.

If the opponent you are pushing moves one of his feet to compensate for or to regain lost balance, he will not be furthering his ability to neutralize an attack by a well-timed shift of his body. In addition, the moment he takes a step will be a moment of vulnerability and could be exploited in a fighting situation by a quick finger stab to the eyes or some other effective and decisive offensive or defensive tactic. When an opponent moves his feet to avoid being pushed, his actions could be construed as indicating that we have moved on to a different kind of sparring and are no longer bound by our agreed upon attempt to confine ourselves to the patterns of movement dictated by tai chi and Taoist principles. Resisting a push also falls into the foregoing category, because by resisting we also break with the principles of tai chi chuan, fail to practice the all-important neutralization, and in the moment of resistance are in a static position, vulnerable to the opponent's succeeding attack.

However, because our primary goal in push-hands is not fighting, we need not react to a breach of the rules in the more extreme way described above. The opponent's reactions might be interpreted more liberally as merely an inability to neutralize correctly and an attempt to somehow cope with loss, or potential loss, of balance. We should then simply continue our attack in the restrained way suggested above.

As for the quality of your finishing technique, an important consideration in fighting because you do not want your opponent to merely shrug off your efforts and return undamaged to the fray, your training should have given you the ability to transmit the energy generated by your feet, legs, and waist through your upper body and arms onto the target in the proportions you choose. At the instant your light push or your neutralization has caused your opponent to momentarily lose his balance, you are afforded options ranging from a decisive punch or strike aimed at a vulnerable area of the opponent's body to a lock or injurious pressure on a joint. Examples are: If the opponent has overextended and straightened his arms, you might catch his hand and apply a wristlock. (FIGURES 75 and 76.) The overextension might result in an elbow dislocation. (FIGURES 77 and 78.) If the opponent's arm is extended and has been caught in an

FIGURE 75

FIGURE 76

FIGURE 77

FIGURE 78

FIGURE 79

FIGURE 80

arm bar, his attempt to free his arm could result in a shoulder lock. (FIGURES 79 and 80.) Missing the center and extending the pushing hand could allow an edge of hand throat strike. (FIGURES 81 and 82.)

Although my emphasis in push-hands is not on its fighting aspect, tai chi chuan is a fighting system and I see no value in watering down its various elements to the point where its practice differs little from dance. Therefore, always be mindful of the potential for effective attack and defense as you practice, reducing your vulnerability and in some way exploiting the opponent's at every opportunity.

FIGURE 81

FIGURE 82

10. Remain Rooted

Rootedness is an important part of a correct tai chi stance. But you should not confuse the concept of rootedness with taking a strong position with your legs and hips in order to resist your opponent's push. Many students neutralize pushes by withdrawing a certain distance and then resisting the push by bracing and taking the force into their rooted back leg. (FIGURE 83.) If the attacker continues to apply force in the same direction, the defender may be able to rotate his body and turn the incoming force to one side or the other, causing the attacker to lose balance. (FIGURES 84 and 85.) Of course, these methods violate tai chi principles in that both attacker and defender oppose strength with strength. The defender should have attempted to neutralize the attacking push in some other way than by this kind of resistance, or misunderstood rooting. The attacker should have changed the direction of his push the instant he sensed resistance from the defender. (see #4.)

FIGURE 83

FIGURE 84

FIGURE 85

FIGURE 86

It is unfortunate when mistaken approaches to push-hands like this concept of rootedness prove effective against opponents. Success will encourage the continued use of a method that is essentially flawed because it depends on the opponent's use of strength in his attack along one single direction. If the attacker suddenly changed the direction of his attack, the defender's root would no longer serve as a resistance foundation. Of course, if the attacker is pushing with equal strength in both hands, a poor method because there is then little chance to vary timing and amount of energy transmitted by each hand, then the root will serve the defender quite well. Having made the error of using both hands at the same time, the attacker will feel that he has hit a wall. He would do well to withdraw and go on the defensive. Were he to increase the strength of his push, the defender would easily be able to turn him aside.

A variation of the foregoing way of rooting is to offer the opponent a point of resistance as he pushes. (FIGURE 86.) If the attacker fails to follow the tai chi principle of avoiding the use

FIGURE 87

of strength and pushes harder, the defender can suddenly relax, causing the attacker to overextend and to lose his balance or become vulnerable to a counterattack. (FIGURE 87.) This ploy may at first glance seem of value, but it will not work against a more skillful opponent who will not push harder into resistance but will immediately switch the attack to his other hand. Therefore, you will further your development if you avoid resistance for any reason and concentrate instead on denying the opponent a sense of your center's location.

The correct way of rooting is to keep your feet firmly in place, allowing your weight to sink into your feet and keeping the rest of your body from the ankles up flexible. My teacher, Cheng, Man-ching, likened rootedness to the behavior of a Daruma doll, which is weighted at its base and tends to give way when pushed at waist level or higher. Avoid, therefore, any resistance to the opponent's push by flexibly shifting your body and moving your center, causing the opponent to lose track of the target, overextend, or otherwise become vulnerable to a counterattack.

11. Maintain the Flow of the Action

One of the Taoist philosophical principles, found in other philosophical systems as well, is that the world around us is in constant flux. Underlying this changing scene there are constants, but the surface change of everything is most noticeable and attracts our attention. Tai chi chuan in its individual form practice reflects the changing nature of the world as one movement seems to end only to become the beginning of the subsequent movement.

In push-hands also you should avoid letting the action stop until either you or your opponent loses balance or is pushed. When attacking keep your body moving forward, changing your push from hand to hand as you detect changes in the opponent's defense. Sometimes an attacker will lose the defender's center and may stop pushing and hold position for a few moments. In this situation, the *Classics* say you should stop as well and wait until the attack resumes. No doubt, waiting for the attack to continue avoids giving the opponent a move of yours to react to or take advantage of. This is generally good advice, but I have found that a very light and carefully executed lateral push is usually successful in turning the situation to your advantage. Of course, as the defender in these circumstances you should already have mounted a counterattack the instant the attacker lost your center. But if you were late in countering and the attack stalled, your lateral counterattack will force the attacker to respond in some way, by neutralizing or resisting it and attempting to continue his attack. In any event, the action and flow will continue once again and you may well now be in control. Remember, all of these actions will take place in split seconds and the advantage will probably be on the side of the defender, given that the attacker momentarily lost his bearings.

The attacker may stop pushing for reasons other than losing your center. For example, he may feel that he is in control and is pausing to allow you to make some additional mistake. This is insufficient reason for his stopping the flow and could give you time to move your center and/or to attempt a counter. At any rate, if you continue to move the attacker will have to resume his attack.

12. Avoid Double-weighting

"Double-weighting" is a term applied to having your weight distributed equally between both feet. (FIGURE 88.) This weight distribution results in a stagnant position or one in which you will have difficulty in performing any sort of effective action. In tai chi the body weight is usually more on one foot than the other, depending on what you wish to do. As you move from one foot to the other, however, your weight will momentarily be equally distributed between both feet. This is a moment of weakness that an alert and skillful opponent can use to disturb your balance. The favored method is for the defender to push the attacker laterally at the very instant the latter, who is moving forward, comes to a 50/50 weight distribution. (see #2.) (FIGURE 89.)

FIGURE 88

FIGURE 89

FIGURE 90

FIGURE 91

Double-weighting sometimes refers to pushing with equal strength in both arms. Push with one hand at a time. (see #4.)

Still another kind of double-weighting occurs when almost all of your weight is on one foot and you push with the hand on that side of the body. Such a push will be ineffective and, because your center of gravity will be mainly over one foot, your balance can be easily disturbed. (FIGURE 90.) Although it is true that one of your feet should bear more weight than the other, avoid making moves where almost all of your weight is on one foot. Also, pushes are correctly done when the arm on the opposite side of the full leg is used. That is, if more of your weight is on your right foot you should push with your left hand. (FIGURE 91.) If the situation suddenly changes and you have to switch to your right hand while your right foot is weighted or full, a slight thrust with the left leg downward combined with a small hip

FIGURE 92

rotation will allow you to switch to your right hand. (FIGURE 92.) Keep in mind, that these pushes are delicately and not powerfully performed.

13. Breathe Correctly

Keep your breathing regular and even, and imagine it going to the *tan t'ien*. A relaxed body will go a long way toward allowing you to breathe in this way. Exhale when you expend effort in your pushing. However, avoid exhaling completely at any time, because if you suddenly have to make a move and have little air in your lungs you will first have to take a short breath in order to respond. This inhalation takes a fraction of a second, but this delay is enough to produce a failed offense or defense. An alert opponent may notice that you have exhaled completely and may choose that moment to attack or counterattack.

Although you can't think about your breathing when you are pushing, if you notice that you are breathing incorrectly, you will have to give it some attention until the problem is solved.

14. Refine Your Movements

When you are first introduced to push-hands, though the more experienced students or teachers will be moving slowly, you will think everything is happening much too fast. This sensation will cause you to make large, wild or only semicontrolled movements in your efforts to catch up. Your movements will also be too big when you try too hard, another common beginner's fault. For a long time you will continue to overreact and overextend, usually losing your balance in the process. Gradually, however, you will notice opportunities and dangers early enough to be able to respond in time and with smaller movements. Help this process along by attempting to refine your movements to make them ever smaller.

15. Keep Your Movements Circular

Movements in the tai chi form and in push-hands generally follow a circular pattern. In pushing, the action may sometimes go in a linear direction, but this linearity usually is the culmination of a preceding circularity. Circularity of movement is especially pertinent in defending against this seeming linear push. If you simply withdraw along one straight line in an attempt to neutralize a push, the attacker will have little trouble following you until you reach the limit of your withdrawal and lose balance or resist. A slight rotation of your body as you withdraw to your back foot may cause the opponent to momentarily lose your center and allow you to counter. This is one instance of the circular patterns apparent in all aspects of push-hands.

Another example of the use of circularity in dealing with a linear attack occurs when your opponent pushes too hard or is exclusively focused on your side as a target. A body rotation will cause him to miss your center and allow you to counter. (FIGURES 93 and 94.) If self-defense were involved you could

FIGURE 93

FIGURE 94

strike his collarbone. (FIGURE 95.) If he had pushed lightly on your side or arm, he would have noticed your rotation attempt at neutralization and could have switched his attack to your chest with his other hand. This point also illustrates the value of pushing lightly over using too much strength.

FIGURE 95

16. Use Your Eyes Correctly

When attacking and facing the opponent squarely, look at his upper chest, a few inches below his chin. (See the many figures showing a correct attacking position.) The object is not to actually see what is there but to avoid looking down or at what your hands or the opponent's hands are doing. Looking down tends to drop your head forward and could well make you lean slightly forward, contributing to your pushing with your arms and shoulders instead of from your legs and hips. Also, watching hands will focus your attention on a specific area, making it likely that you will miss developments in other, and perhaps more important, aspects of your push. Your eyes should, then, not focus on anything but should simply help your system to register whatever happens and to react as seems warranted.

In defending, your body will usually be at an angle to the opponent, making it both difficult and unnecessary to keep your gaze on the upper chest. But, again, try not to "look" at anything.

Avoid, also, closing your eyes in push-hands. You may think that by closing your eyes you will become more efficient in using other sensing equipment, but in my experience this development fails to occur. Your sight may need to work along, harmoniously, with your other senses if you are to notice a shift in your opponent's position, a slight loss of balance on your or the opponent's part, or whatever, in time for you to react correctly. Removing a component of this harmonious interplay of senses may detract from rather than enhance your practice.

Though slightly off the point, a related idea concerning the Taoist approach to meditation has some relevance. It is said that we should not shut out the world around us and focus only inwardly. Rather, focus is alternately inward and outward or, if possible, simultaneously inward and outward. So, keep your eyes open.

X.
Training Tips

N MY EXPERIENCE, students make optimum progress in tai chi when they hold certain respectful attitudes toward their teacher, fellow students and *dojo* (training hall), and maintain generally restrained behavior. Our development over time will probably move us naturally in the directions I am going to suggest, but beginners are best served by having to follow some established forms of behavior as well as by being made aware of preferred ways of interacting with others in the dojo. However, we must be careful not to confuse the sensible requirements for behavior that will help us develop in our art with the way of acting typical of the culture or society from which we borrowed it. For example, as Americans we need not behave toward one another in the Confucian or hierarchical way Chinese or Japanese culture might dictate. On the other hand, our individualistic, informal, egalitarian way of interacting also needs modification if our training is to bring about in us beneficial change.

To begin with, we should regard the *dojo* as a special place where we meet to work on developing ourselves. In more formal training halls, students bow to the hall and to the teacher when they enter and leave. They are usually required to leave their outdoor footgear at the door. Usually, also, students change clothing, although the demands of a martial art like judo for clothing that can withstand rough treatment is more responsible for what is worn than is an attempt at mood change or costume standardization. Finally, loudness and boisterousness are discouraged in favor of decorum and restraint, because such excessive behavior disturbs the climate helpful for developing a settled equanimity.

In assessing students' attitude, level of development, and character, teachers note seemingly inconsequential actions such as lateness in coming to class and missing scheduled classes. Teachers usually are of the opinion that if students really want to attend class and to be on time, they will not be absent or late. Naturally, a rare absence or lateness (perhaps once in six months) is understandable, but frequent lapses of this sort will not go unnoticed or unremarked. Students may think holding them to such standards reflects rigidity and diminishes their adulthood. But if students do a bit of probing into their true attitudes about being on time or avoiding absences, they may well uncover their underlying belief that tai chi practice and its influence on their life is less important to them than something else. The "something else" may just be a difficulty in overcoming inertia, not wishing to be rushed or poor planning rather than a specific other interest. They may also notice that their behavior may reflect a self-centeredness, a desire to be noticed, or a disregard for or unconcern for the agreement between themselves and their teacher and their fellow students, made at the outset of training, that they would attend class regularly and avoid lateness.

Students may argue that in missing class or coming late they are following the tai chi principles of not hurrying, of leaving things undone, or of not doing too much. Unfortunately, teachers will classify such arguments under rationalizations, and will try to make students more aware of the requirements of their training and of the training's reflection in their daily life.

Another aspect of our training concerns how we relate to teachers. Certainly we need not exhibit toward them the rather extreme veneration we sometimes see among Asians. Yet the fact remains that something out of the ordinary is going on, and that we are indebted to our teachers, because they are usually sharing with us their expertise in an art which, practiced diligently, can help us to see things more clearly. Paying for this training with money goes only part of the way on the road of properly discharging our debt. We have additional obligations to our teachers and foremost among them is for us to do our best to learn what is taught and to put it into practice in our daily lives. Though it may seem a strange concept, probably we cannot ever fully pay the debt we owe our teachers, but we can make some strides in this direction by influencing others through the changes our training has effected in us. On a more demonstrative level, we also owe our teacher a full measure of respect and deference, and Americans will probably feel most comfortable in displaying this attitude in a measured and restrained way.

Many of us may experience difficulty in adopting this general way of thinking about our teachers, because we may view them as "only" human beings, just as we are, not deserving of any special treatment beyond the dictates of politeness. When viewed from the perspective of our trying to avoid getting caught by outward form there is certainly some merit in this point of view. But it should be tempered with the feeling that rises from our realization that our teachers are further along the path than most of us in the direction we all wish to go, and that they can point the way and are willing to do so. Despite any human failings teachers are sure to have, if we focus on the positive aspects of their role we should be able to acknowledge our debt to them and to treat them with greater respect and deference than we might an equal.

Some students will want to know more about their teacher than may be possible in a class setting. They may feel their development on some level will be enhanced by being in his presence. Others may look for opportunities to socialize with the teacher and observe his behavior outside of class, where he is not in control of the proceedings. Still others may wish to observe him more closely in a search for flaws that might serve to reassure themselves of their own worth. Some may even seek a sexual relationship in an effort to know him more intimately and to experience that side of the teacher. Unfortunately, whatever brings teachers and students together outside the dojo where training is replaced by other kinds of interaction tends to undermine the teacher-student relationship. If teachers stop acting as teachers, as is possible and perhaps expected in a social environment, students usually have trouble avoiding some modification of their thinking about what it is they are learning and about their teacher's function. The closer in the usual social sense the relationship between teacher and student becomes, the less able is the teacher to act as a teacher or the student as a student.

How should we behave toward our fellow students? The students who are senior to us, especially where a number of years of training separates us, will help formally teach us and, therefore, on the level of technique correction assume some of the mantle of the teacher. As for students who have studied more or less as long as we, regarding them as siblings, or better yet, as fellow travelers on our common path is most apt. As we advance together, we should expect to help others along and in turn, to be helped by others. Such help may merely take the outward form of providing one another workout partners or opponents in push-hands, but it will also include the support and interchange on deeper levels we all need.

Again, your practice and development will suffer if in pushing you place other desires above internalizing the principles of push-hands. For example, you may be sexually or emotionally attracted to another student and use your time in pushing to make some sort of connection. Even if you do or say nothing overt, your mind will be occupied with thoughts other than those concerned with push-hands. If you view your opponent as a competitor whom you wish to dominate, your pushing may well suffer, because to avoid losing or to win you will resist or use too much strength. Ultimately, any intention you may have concerning your opponent, other than working with each other to further your development, will prevent you from getting the full measure of training from your practice.

Although you need not work on preventing yourself from having thoughts unrelated to push-hands—thoughts will come and go—you can learn to avoid allowing them to catch and hold your attention. If you wish, when push-hands is over, you can give your full attention to anything of importance you may remember occurred to you while pushing. If an idea you had intrigues you, you can attempt to determine its origin and to reflect on it, often with benefit. But while pushing, learn simply to react to what is happening without, at the same time, thinking of something else.

Some ambitious and perhaps accomplished students may feel that pushing hands with those less skillful than themselves will not help them improve, or that they will learn more if they push with opponents of equal or greater skill. But if the more skillful students confine their practice to those on their own level, both they and the less able will lose the benefits both can derive from working with one another. In my experience, students can improve their push-hands even when practicing with those much less skillful than themselves.

Another reason for students not practicing together is that one student may dislike another. This behavior is somewhat misguided, because, aside from the failure to develop the sense of their connectedness with others, through this avoidance they deny themselves the chance for improved knowledge of the person they believe they dislike. Additional knowledge could change dislike into, at least, tolerance. By not pushing they not only miss the chance for more knowledge and better understanding of the other person but also for additional self-understanding. If they practice with everyone they may realize that it is really something in themselves that could be adjusted to allow them to interact more profitably with their fellow students. I cite these few illustrations to make the important point that students should push with all of their fellows and not favor some to the exclusion of others. Of course, we all have our preferences among people and students will be attracted to others of like mind, but they must realize they are in a training hall and that a different set of rules and priorities applies than those they might follow on the outside.

Some students may feel that doing the solo form and pushing hands in the particular way a teacher may prescribe is not bringing them quickly enough to the self-realization goals they have set for themselves. Contributing to the rise of this negative attitude is the fact that substantial changes in our thinking generally come about only over a period of years, causing those impatient for results to doubt the efficacy of their training and to look elsewhere for answers or other approaches. They may turn to the writings of other teachers and, imagining they understand the value of a method they are not presently using, attempt to make changes in their training or, at the least, resist the approach of their teacher. They may also seek out other teachers in the hope of making faster progress or of getting on the right track. Of course, if after a few years of training they become dissatisfied with their teacher, they probably erred in choosing him or her in the first place. In addition, although it is true that students need to find a teacher who is right for them, if they have spent some years with one teacher and become dissatisfied, it is likely that their unhappiness stems mainly from faults in themselves, such as lack of patience and perseverance, or unrealistic expectations rather than from their training method or their teacher's seeming inadequacies.

Related to the foregoing point is a final word concerning students who have heard or read that an art like tai chi chuan has secret methods to which only those a teacher favors are privy. Books refer to special diets, medicines, or other aids to help development. Some say teachers hold back some ultimate knowledge or technique to maintain an edge over even their most accomplished students. All these ideas are nonsense. Good teachers will invariably, over the years, share all of their knowledge with their students. The problem is that students have to be at a level, or developed enough, to be able to receive this transmission. Then they have to practice for some years to internalize the knowledge, to make it their own. So there is a secret but it is so simple and straightforward that most will not believe it and will spend their time looking for it ever further afield. The secret is practice.